MORE QUICK HITS

MORE QUICK HITS

Successful Strategies by Award-Winning Teachers

Edited by

S. Holly Stocking

Eileen T. Bender

Claude H. Cookman

J. Vincent Peterson

Robert B. Votaw

With the editorial assistance of

Karen Everdon

Angie Wu

INDIANA UNIVERSITY PRESS

Bloomington • Indianapolis

This book is a publication of

Indiana University Press
601 North Morton Street
Bloomington, IN 47404-3797 USA

http://www.indiana.edu/~iupress

Telephone orders 800-842-6796
Fax orders 812-855-7931
Orders by e-mail iuporder@indiana.edu

The paper used in this publication meets the minimum requirements of American National Standard for Information Sciences—Permanence of Paper for Printed Library Materials, ANSI Z39.48-1984.

Manufactured in the United States of America

Library of Congress Cataloging-in-Publication Data

More quick hits : successful strategies by award-winning teachers / edited by S. Holly Stocking . . . [et al.] ; editorial assistance by Karen Everdon, Angie Wu.
   p. cm.
"Sequel to Quick hits"—Introd.
  Includes bibliographical references.
  ISBN 0-253-21238-3 (pbk. : alk. paper)
  1. College teaching—Indiana—Case studies. 2. College teachers—Indiana—Case studies. 3. Indiana University—Faculty. I. Stocking, S. Holly. II. Quick Hits
LB2331.M58 1998
378.1'25'09772—dc21   98-20679

  1 2 3 4 5 03 02 01 00 99 98

4

Contents

5

7. Using assessment and evaluation for learning 92

8. Learning to teach and teaching to learn 116

7

8

Foreword

Good teaching is hard work. No one better knows that than good teachers, which is why they are constantly on the lookout for ways to improve what they teach, how they teach, and especially how students learn.

Good teachers are thoughtful and reflective; they go beyond rote transmission of information. They are open to new ideas and innovative approaches, and they realize that they can gain from the experience and expertise of others.

In fact, good teachers are great learners. Not only do they master a given subject, they also throw themselves into the study of new methods of presentation, including the best uses of the growing number of information technology tools. They understand that they are members of a learning community, and they welcome the opportunities it provides.

More Quick Hits provides for an exchange of successful ideas and methods for good teaching. I compliment FACET for originating this mode of exchange, and I commend the authors for their originality and wisdom in developing good teaching techniques and for their willingness to share them with others. In doing so, they have fostered one of the most exciting aspects of a genuine learning community: the free and open exchange of ideas.

Myles Brand, President, Indiana University

Introduction

More Quick Hits is the sequel to *Quick Hits*, a popular book of teaching tips developed by some of Indiana University's most talented teachers.

The original *Quick Hits* grew out of the annual retreats of FACET (the Faculty Colloquium on Excellence in Teaching), an organization established in 1989 to recognize and support distinguished teaching faculty from each of IU's eight campuses, and to provide a forum for the discussion of teaching and university policy.

Beginning with the third annual retreat, new inductees into FACET were invited to bring their favorite teaching strategies and explain or demonstrate them in three- to five-minute blocks interspersed between longer workshops. So lively, entertaining, and valuable were these "hits" that they quickly became a regular feature of the annual retreats. The original *Quick Hits*, published in 1994 by Indiana University Press, circulated these and other classroom-tested ideas to college and university teachers beyond our own campuses and instantly became a best-selling volume. Indeed, the popularity of *Quick Hits* far surpassed everyone's expectations, reaching colleges and universities not only in our 50 United States, but around the globe. Teachers clearly were hungry for strategies that would help them do a better job.

What's new

This sequel extends the original volume's reach to include the successful teaching strategies of IU's award-winning teachers outside the FACET network and of others selected because they are extraordinarily talented supporters of the teaching mission at our university.

More Quick Hits also attempts, in a modest way, to shift our focus from our own teaching to our students' learning. When we made our call for submissions, we asked teachers for strategies that they have used successfully to promote and ensure students' learning. This emphasis on learning—rather than teaching—reflects a subtle but profound shift in thinking about education that is influencing classroom activities at all levels.

What's here

The resulting contributions include, in addition to the kinds of traditional classroom activities we have come to expect in such volumes, tips for organizing courses and creating genuine learning communities where students and teachers learn together. They include tips for involving students more actively in their own learning—in developing syllabi and examinations, for example, or in constructively evaluating one another's work. They include strategies for dealing with students' emotions, diverse backgrounds, and various learning styles, which can seriously challenge our old ways of doing things. In addition, they include tips for harnessing technologies to ensure learning, for using community service for learning, and for shaping writing assignments and testing for learning. They also include ways to foster critical and creative thinking, and to help students learn about learning itself.

Out of our belief that teachers must be included in the learning equation, we also have included a section on learning to teach. This section includes not only "quick hits" for those new to teaching or for those new to different kinds of instruction, like team-teaching, but it also includes a few "quick slips," stories of mistakes that teachers have made and learned from in their teaching. The volume contains a "quick list" of weightier books and articles that some of us have found valuable resources for our own learning about teaching. Finally, sprinkled throughout the book, are some "quick wits," little words of wisdom or humor about teaching and learning that have inspired us or made us smile.

Why the shift to learning is important

Alas, learning—our students' and our own—is something too many of us have taken for granted. Our university president, Myles Brand, likes to tell the story about the professor who came out of a class thinking he had done the best class of his entire career; the slides were right; the jokes were well timed; everything worked. "The trouble is," the professor complained, "the students just didn't get it." The trouble is, our president likes to say, that professor didn't get it. If the students weren't learning, he wasn't teaching!

It is a working assumption of *More Quick Hits* that if our students are not learning, we are not teaching. We might add, if we as teachers are not continually learning—about our subject, and about teaching and learning, both—we are failing to impart to our students the greatest lesson of all: The best among us never stop learning—from texts and images, from personal experiences, and perhaps most importantly, from one another.

S. Holly Stocking, Journalism, IU Bloomington

11

1 Designing courses and environments for learning

Courses have architectures. There's the architecture of the classroom, the architecture of the syllabus, and the architecture of lectures and activities. How do we become architects of courses and environments that inspire and promote learning? If you're Sharon Hamilton, you create an agenda. If you're Glenn Gass, you construct a course on a foundation of love: You teach a subject that has been a life-long passion. Others of us have mixed levels of students in the same classroom or created mini-courses that help older students study abroad despite their work and family obligations. Classroom architecture is something we don't often talk about as teachers, but ought to. In this section, a few of our contributors have.

Too much fun to be work?

I am fortunate enough to teach a subject—The History of Rock Music—that has been a lifelong passion, and the quickest hit I could offer from my own experience is to advise every teacher to find a way to teach what he or she truly loves. This may be easier said than done, but one should never assume that it can't happen or be afraid of an unexpected change of direction. I certainly could not have imagined that my years of training as a classical composer would lead me to the job that I have now, or that Indiana University's School of Music—a noble bastion of the Great Tradition—would ever approve the idea of offering courses on rock 'n' roll. Even after the courses were approved and a part of the curriculum, it took me several years to realize that I had created a "Dream Job," rather than a temporary bridge between graduate school and a "real" job teaching serious music.

I have finally realized that it is okay to have fun teaching and to blur the distinctions between work and play, or "research" and pleasure, and I am now certain that I would be a hopelessly ineffectual teacher if I could not look at every class as an opportunity to share something that is important to me on a personal level. This direct emotional involvement leads naturally to an enthusiasm in the classroom that really does seem contagious and essential for engaging student interest. (I can hardly ask my students to get excited if I can't.) For that reason, I am always happiest when a student comments favorably on my enthusiasm for teaching, as I have come to view "enthusiasm" and "effectiveness" as nearly synonymous.

> *I have finally realized that it is okay to have fun teaching and to blur the distinctions between work and play, or 'research' and pleasure.*

Glenn Gass, Music, IU Bloomington

Collaborative syllabus

The scope of the natural sciences is expanding rapidly, so rapidly that it is impossible to cover all the principles and content that we would like to include in a single semester. How do we choose which topics to include and which to leave out? We certainly cannot expect our students to learn more content than they did five or 10 years ago. We could sort the content by our own interests and research background. However, available research suggests that we can raise our students' interest and participation if we give them an opportunity to take part in the course design. I have had success with this mode of developing the syllabi for both an introductory earth science class and an advanced course in paleontology.

On the first day of class, I give the students a list of topics that we could cover in the course and ask them to rank no more than 15 of the topics. After class, I compile and weight their preferences according to the number of students who want to discuss or investigate each topic. At the next class meeting, I present the results to the class as a histogram and then give them my proposed set of topics based on their rankings and an appropriate sequence to handle the content. I ask for suggestions for improvement to the syllabus, and if there are none, we collectively agree that the sequence and the content of the syllabus will be the course outline.

I find that students' interests and discussions are improved with this method of setting my courses' syllabi. Their willingness to read more outside of class is greatly increased, and, in a dynamic subject like earth science, there is always something of interest.

In my paleontology class, I go a step further and put students with the same interests into teams to study the fossil record of organisms that they personally find intriguing. The students are expected to report to the class at end of the semester about their findings. This gives them an added incentive to use our fossil collection, do research in the library, and make an oral presentation to their peers. I have found these strategies to be very successful in my classes, with increased student interest and participation in their own learning processes.

Robert B. Votaw, Geosciences, IU Northwest

Facilitating discussion through review

At the start of each class period in my Introduction to Sociology course, we review the previous session's key materials. I tell students to take out their notes and a pen or high-lighter. Then I ask students to answer questions verbally about key points from the previous class. This sets a tone for the class period, which emphasizes the importance of discussion in learning. Since students will, it is hoped, have the necessary information to answer questions in front of them, participation is relatively low risk. This allows students to build the confidence necessary for participation later in the session when they don't have clear answers in front of them. It also allows students to check their note-taking skills. If they have the information we discuss in their notes, they can simply highlight the key points. If not, I encourage them to pay closer attention during class and attempt to focus on the central issues of the class session. Students often remark in their course evaluations that this was one of the aspects of the course they most appreciated.

Jay Howard, Sociology, IUPU Columbus

Chemistry party animals

Many students view chemistry as an arcane science practiced by nerds in white lab coats. This perception often persists even after learning the fundamental concepts of chemistry. The problem, as I see it, is that students have little opportunity in class to connect the concepts and chemical equations to everyday life.

To solve this problem, I have designed an activity in which I relate pH and buffer theory to everyday problems one encounters at parties. I tell the students that they have been invited to a geek party where free food is plentiful. The contents of their stomachs are represented by a beaker containing red cabbage juice. As a pH indicator, red cabbage juice has much more visual impact than litmus paper. (Whoever heard of litmus paper outside a chemistry lab?) As the hypothetical evening progresses, acidic foods are added to the simulated stomach. The changing color of the cabbage juice clearly indicates that acid indigestion looms. Most party-going students know the antidote is an antacid such as Alka-Seltzer. As I add a couple of these to the simulated stomach, the pH becomes less acidic. I remind the class of various television commercials that lend credence to the feeling of relief. I then point out that Alka-Seltzer is a buffer and therefore resists changes in pH. Feeling better, the student in our hypothetical scenario parties some more and ingests more acidic foods. As the cabbage juice in our simulated stomach attests, the antacid continues to resist changes in pH. The party can last well into the wee hours of the morning.

Although I take some liberties (for example, the pH of the stomach is actually much lower than in our simulation), the point is clear. It is then an easy leap to explain how carbonate and phosphate buffers resist changes in pH in the blood and tissues, why lakes lined with buffering limestone resist effects of acid rain, and why ancient marble statues have deteriorated dramatically since the Industrial Revolution.

> *Chemists are nerds? Well, maybe. But few students still consider chemistry the recondite field they originally envisioned.*

Chemists are nerds? Well, maybe. But few students still consider chemistry the recondite field they originally envisioned.

Gretchen Anderson, Chemistry, IU South Bend

Passport for non-traditional students

Our campus is a community university, and most of our students work at least part time, many of them supporting families while going to school. It is therefore very difficult to get them to study abroad for a year, or even a semester, as many do on residential campuses. The expense and time involved are too great for almost all of them. In an effort to provide an opportunity more in line with their possibilities, another faculty member and I developed a Nineteenth Century English History and Culture class to be taught in England during the summer. We designed it so that a segment was taught on our campus for about four weeks (including enough class time to equal about two-thirds of the time spent in an ordinary class). In my case, this was a course on nineteenth century British history. Students had the same number of books to read and the same number of written assignments that my ordinary classes have, and we covered essentially the same material in a somewhat briefer and more selective fashion.

We then flew to England, where we spent three weeks visiting many of the places we had studied. Since much of London was built in the nineteenth century, we spent most of our time there. Other cities we visited included Oxford, High Wycombe, Brighton, and Merthyr Tydfil. We visited homes of major historical figures, Parliament (where we had a personal tour and commentary by an MP), various historical landmarks and locations, and many museums and galleries. In addition to political and economic history, we studied the society, art, and literature of the period. We included attendance at plays, operas, and concerts in our activities. Since there are so many of these in London, we could usually find examples that were appropriate. For their final examination, the students related what they had seen and studied in England and Wales to their more bookish studies at home.

Students had an extra week between their studies in the UK and their finals. Most of them engaged in further travel, some in the UK and some on the continent. Sometimes I

15

conducted these classes on my own; when I was joined by another professor, the students took two classes. In one case, for example, they took my course in addition to a course in British politics. Another pair of professors combined history with literature in the same historical period.

To keep expenses as low as possible, I made group arrangements for travel and lodging. This enabled us to charge far less than any other such program with which I am familiar. We have stayed in dormitories (many are vacant during the summer), apartments (I found some for as little as $20 per person per night—very nice ones, too!), and bed and breakfast houses. Public transportation passes enabled us to travel freely through central London at a very reasonable rate. On a typical day, we spent about six to seven hours visiting sites, including travel time. Students had the rest of the day for study or other activities. Sundays they had off, with optional trips to historic churches.

These classes were a great deal of work. I have never been willing to schedule them less than five years apart. But they have been very rewarding, both for me and for the students.

Paul H. Scherer, History, IU South Bend

Mixing student levels can improve discussion

In our department, we often teach courses on the same topic, taught at different levels and meeting simultaneously. Usually, these combine a freshman/sophomore with a junior/senior class and sometimes a graduate level as well. The levels differ in reading assignments, written work, and examinations, but they have the same lectures and/or discussions. These classes have usually been quite successful, particularly when the approach is primarily or exclusively discussion.

When I first taught this type of class, I was concerned that the introductory-level students might be intimidated by being placed in a class with more advanced students. This did not turn out to be a problem, perhaps because I assigned different books for the students at different levels. This gave each group a monopoly on certain information, which they could then contribute to the discussions. As each group was bringing in different information, the discussions were enriched. Class participation and enthusiasm were also improved by the selection of books reflecting differing interpretations. For example, in my Cold War courses, some books are by revisionists, some by traditionalists, and some by those who take a neutral position. I often throw in a provocative work, such as *The Origins of the Second World War* by A. J. P. Taylor, balanced with careful, more traditional accounts.

> *I have found that a blend of straight factual questions and interpretative or 'iffy' questions works well.*

Students receive a list of questions for the next week in order to enable them to prepare in advance for the multilevel discussions. I have found that a blend of straight factual questions and interpretative or "iffy" questions works well. An example of the latter is the following: "Was Churchill's deal with Stalin about the partition of the Balkans into spheres of influence wise? Should Roosevelt have assisted Churchill and thereby obtained a better deal?" This approach allows for systematic, but nevertheless interesting, coverage

16

of the topics. Students have ample opportunity to raise their own questions as well.

I select examination questions from previously assigned discussion questions so that there are no surprises. Most students do quite well, both in discussion and in examinations.

In my experience, the narrower the topic (within reason), the better these techniques work. I would not use them, for example, in a Western Civilization course. However, I have used them successfully in an honors course in Twentieth Century World History and find them to be ideal for my diplomatic history classes.

Paul H. Scherer, History, IU South Bend

Agenda for the classroom

Microsoft Word has just helped me become a better teacher. Or, to be more accurate, the Microsoft Agenda Wizard, a recent workshop on "Achieving Excellence through Collaborative Problem-Solving: Effective Facilitation A Critical Tool," and dozens upon dozens of meetings have led me to a seemingly obvious insight: Running an effective classroom has a lot of similarities to running an effective meeting.

When you plan a meeting, you think of what needs to be accomplished, what the participants need in order to accomplish the tasks, and what steps need to be taken in order to accomplish the tasks. Secondarily, you consider how long each of these steps will take and plan your agenda accordingly. Your experience tells you that a well-planned agenda often results in a well-executed meeting. The Microsoft Agenda Wizard even leaves space to designate who is responsible for any follow-up action items. Everyone is focused; everyone knows what needs to be accomplished; and everyone knows what is expected of him or her within what time frame.

Juxtaposing the format of the Microsoft Agenda Wizard with lessons learned from "Achieving Excellence through Collaborative Problem-Solving" (a workshop on effective facilitation by Angotti Weber and Associates), I have developed an effective agenda for the classroom. It can be given in hard copy to students before the class begins, written on the board as the class progresses, or a combination of those techniques:

Objectives for the class: This focuses the class on what you and they are supposed to accomplish.

Outline of major topics for discussion: Often we assume that students automatically connect discussion with objectives for the class. These connections may be made more explicit in this format.

Approximate time for each topic: Often the heat of discussion leads us away from our objectives and leaves insufficient time. (Of course, these digressions are the sparks that often inflame the learning spirit.) Estimating time, with built-in safeguards for spontaneous excitement, helps keep both students and professors on track.

Opportunities to check understanding: In the passion of transmitting our wisdom and insights to students, we may assume understanding where there is some confusion. If you plan for checks of understanding for two or three of the most difficult concepts soon after talking about them, you may minimize potential confusion and clarify understanding. Two easy ways to do this are the following:

   1. **The one-minute essay.** Students write or apply the concept and then share with another student; differences are discussed and questions raised where necessary.

2. The one-minute chat session. Students in pairs summarize the concept in their own words or apply it to a new situation or problem.

Follow-up for retention and extension: This may take several forms: Writing or reading assignments, suggested activities, or an entry into new work. Making explicit the connections between the class work and the follow-up work helps students understand the significance of homework assignments.

Closure: Before the class ends, return to your class objectives and main topics. On occasion, you might ask students to write for one minute about whether the class objectives were met. Another strategy for closure is to have students write down any questions they have about the concepts or procedures of the class. You can then answer these questions at the beginning of the next class.

The benefits: The many benefits include explicit connections between each class, recapitulation of important concepts from previous class, opportunities to clarify potential confusion, a strong signal to students that confusion is a necessary part of learning and that students' questions play a significant role in the learning of the entire class.

Adjournment!

Sharon Hamilton, English, IUPUI

Language-learning and student involvement

As a beginning teacher, I believed that it was my presentation of grammar, vocabulary, and cultural context that were most critical for successful student learning of Japanese. Gradually, however, I came to understand that something else mattered more—student involvement in the learning process. There is no denying that the teacher's mastery of the material, a well-planned syllabus, and clearly structured class sessions are essential to constructing a positive environment for language-learning, but daily and meaningful student involvement seems to be the key. This insight has had important consequences for the way in which I now prepare for and conduct class. Let me briefly mention three.

First, the time I invest in class preparation is spent, not so much in reviewing the material that will be covered in the next day's class, but in devising and refining exercises that teach the material through student participation. Over the years, I have been able to develop a collection of particularly effective exercises for each aspect of language instruction, and I revise and add more each semester.

Every indication is given to the students that the class revolves around their participation.

Second, during class, little time is allotted to formal explanation of the material, but great attention is paid to each student's execution of the exercises. For example, while I may offer a brief explanation of the difference between the particle that indicates "place of existence" (*ni*) and the one designating "place of action" (*de*), most of the class is devoted to working through exercises that make this distinction clear. The focuses of class work are the teacher-student and student-student interactions when they are paired in teams.

Third, from the very beginning of the course, every indication is given to the students that the class revolves around their participation. They speak from the first moments of

18

the first session, I give daily quizzes, and short homework assignments are almost as frequent. When the proper tone is set, the minds of all participants in the process naturally center on the tasks at hand.

An early Chinese text describes the manner and impact of the Taoist sage as follows: "Hesitant, they do not utter words lightly. When their task is accomplished and their work done, the people all say, 'It happened to us naturally.'" The language teacher may have to utter more words than the Taoist sage, but by stressing student involvement, the desired outcome, I believe, is the same: Before the students know it, they have learned.

Yasuko Ito Watt, East Asian Languages and Cultures, IU Bloomington

Top ten lists

Finance is a difficult subject and at times can be quite dry. Real life examples and cases can help bring it to life, but one of the best ways that I have found to keep the students alert and interested is the occasional use of humor. Not all of us are comedians, and some of us are even comically challenged, but using a "Top Ten List" takes no special talent. I have found this technique not only popular, but useful to demonstrate and reinforce financial concepts.

Top Ten Lists originated with David Letterman's "Late Night" television show. They typically consist of 10 related one-line jokes that are read in reverse order, leading up to No. 1 so that the humor builds. The list often works because it moves so quickly that the next item is up before the students have had the chance to reflect on the possible lack of humor in the previous item. Students will often volunteer a drum roll on the top of their desk if you pause before No 1.

> *Not all of us are comedians, and some of us are even comically challenged, but using a 'Top Ten List' takes no special talent.*

Students often find it easier to remember financial principles that they have laughed at as part of a Top Ten List. Popular lists I've used have included: "Top Ten List of Finance Principles," "Top Ten Financial Ratios," "Top Ten Ways to Lower the Cost of Capital," "Top Ten Capital Budgeting Decisions," and "Top Ten Reasons to Know Algebra."

One does need to be careful that students do not take you too seriously. Some may try to write down any list of 10 items for fear it could appear as an exam question. This can be a problem especially with accounting students who tend to take themselves pretty seriously. The following is one of the first Top Ten Lists that I have used to alleviate this problem:

Top Ten reasons why students fail finance

10. Finance is boring.
9. I didn't buy the Study Guide in order to save money.
8. I didn't do all the homework problems in order to save time.
7. The teacher is boring.
6. What homework problems?
5. My solar calculator wouldn't work in the dimly lit classroom.

19

4. There are more formulas in corporate finance than in the baby food aisle at the grocery store.

3. Michael Milliken studied finance, and look where he wound up.

2. Unless "present value" has something to do with my birthday, I don't see why it's important.

And, the number one reason on the Top Ten List of Why Students Fail Finance:

1. I discovered my true interest is in the Arts.

Dianne Roden, Finance, IU Kokomo

The compleat discussion section

These suggestions combine some long-held views of teaching and some ideas I have encountered more recently and am still experimenting with. The first seven items go through a teaching chronology of planning, performing, and evaluating. Later items stand on their own.

1. Think carefully about your audience and try to find out where they really are. Our students vary tremendously, but as a group they differ from us significantly in experience, analytic skills, sophistication, and cultural attitudes. The more we understand that, the more of what we value can be transmitted. Missing this, we risk going over their heads or—if we overcompensate—becoming condescending.

2. Begin planning your sections by writing out goals that are concrete and phrased in terms of student experience. In other words, not "Teach them how great *Frankenstein* is," but more like this: "Have them think about what it is about this story that has fascinated so many readers and film directors."

3. Design activities that will achieve those goals with that audience. Again, put it in writing, at least in shorthand: "Briefly remind them of the book's amazing durability and of the many films it has inspired." Break into groups of four. Have them spend five minutes individually brainstorming on paper about what the attraction might be. Include movies they have seen. Discuss and sift in groups for 10 minutes, choosing one favorite idea in each group. Discuss favorites as a class, encouraging clarity and individuality of interpretation. Every minute you spend in this kind of clarification will pay off for you and your students.

4. Frame activities at the beginning. Unless there is a good reason to surprise students, tell them at the beginning generally what you are up to and why: "Very popular cultural images and stories, if we look at them carefully, can tell us important things about our culture that otherwise are hard to see. Today we're going to do some exercises that will help us understand what is so appealing about Mary Shelley's 180-year-old story and what that suggests about our own culture."

5. Get feedback. Before class, ask yourself how you will know whether you have achieved your goals, and devise a way to check. It could involve asking the students directly what they learned or asking them to write something that will show whether they have learned what you expected them to.

6. Frame it at the end. Conclude with comments suggesting the relation of the day's discoveries to culture more generally and to course themes. Also comment briefly on any interesting class dynamics and perhaps on something you learned in class.

7. Be sure to save time for framing and other shaping. Avoid classes that just go until the time is up and then stop.

8. Evaluate yourself constructively. After class, make brief notes to yourself on successes and mistakes, ideas for the next time you teach that subject, and how to lead from that to what comes next. Get student feedback often, and arrange to have someone with an interest in pedagogy visit your class a couple of times in the first month of the semester and maybe once at midpoint.

9. In everything you do in the classroom, be aware of the level of your students' attention. If it isn't what you'd like, think about doing something else—or "doing the same thing differently."

10. Also watch your own level of effort. If you are working hard, you are probably trying to do your students' work for them. Relax, review, and rerun with yourself out of the spotlight.

11. Show respect for students who are trying, regardless of their level of comprehension, and do not tolerate students' lack of respect for each other, for course materials, or for you. Humor and redirection can sometimes help block an undesirable development.

12. One form of respect in discussion is taking class participation seriously. Tell students at the start that you expect them to talk in class and that discussion can be exploratory so their comments do not have to be perfect or final. Call on non-volunteers regularly from the beginning, and take their contributions as constructively as possible. Don't leave a contributor hanging; try to take each comment somewhere before you look for more.

13. Value difference of opinion and background, and bring it to the foreground when it seems interesting, linking it to your model of interpretation. I have found it helpful to make a distinction between two things that can happen in discussion: "argument," whose goal is to disprove or invalidate the other, and "discussion," whose goal is to explore and understand the other. Both have their place, but while many students come to the university well prepared to argue, few will "discuss" without coaching and support.

14. Think of yourself at all times as a teacher: someone who enables students to learn and change, rather than a sorter who grades students on what they came in with.

15. Regularly model the skills your students will be graded on.

16. Rather than the "talking expert," think of yourself as a designer of environments that facilitate learning. In the classroom, the ones who are working are the ones who are learning. Design situations and activities that will lead your students to do the work that will accomplish your teaching goals.

> *Think of yourself as a designer of environments that facilitate learning.*

John A. Woodcock, English, IU Bloomington

The power of the bad example

There is nothing like the power of the bad example to promote learning.

I began to understand this after I joined an African-American choral ensemble conducted by a gifted teacher. If we moved our lips incorrectly, he would good-naturedly exaggerate our mistake with his own lips and say, "Not this." Then, in an instant, he would smile broadly and, modeling the correct way to do what he wanted, he would say, "What you need to do is this!" If we involved our shoulders in incorrect ways when breathing with our diaphragms, he made his own large body shake like Santa Claus.

We would laugh at the absurdity of ourselves before he showed us how to sing from our diaphragms correctly.

"You look like this," he would say, and we would laugh at the absurdity of ourselves before he showed us how to sing from our diaphragms correctly.

After that, in yoga classes and in learning any number of new tasks from great teachers, I began to notice that the bad example was often as crucial to my learning as the perfect one. The bad example set the good example in sharp relief. It showed what to avoid, which is something that the good example, by itself, could never do.

I have since made it a point to tap the power of the bad example in designing my teaching activities, and it seems to work. Good examples are important, yes, but when coupled with bad ones, they work even better.

S. Holly Stocking, Journalism, IU Bloomington

Quick wits

In some cases we learn more by looking for the answer to a question and not finding it than we do from learning the answer itself.

Lloyd Alexander

The close observer soon discovers that the teacher's task is not to implant facts but to place the subject to be learned in front of the learner and, through sympathy, emotion, imagination, and patience, to awaken in the learner the restless drive for answers and insights which enlarge the personal life and give it meaning.

Nathan Marsh Pusey

Real education consists in drawing the best out of yourself.

Mohandas K. Gandhi

Only people who die very young learn all they really need to know in kindergarten.

Wendy Kaminer

It is the supreme art of the teacher to awaken joy in creative expression and knowledge.

Albert Einstein

How can we help students to understand that the tragedy of life is not death; the tragedy is to die with commitments undefined and convictions undeclared and service unfulfilled?

Vachel Lindsay

A good teacher feels his way, looking for response.

Paul Goodman

I am who we are.

Graffiti, FACET 1998 retreat

23

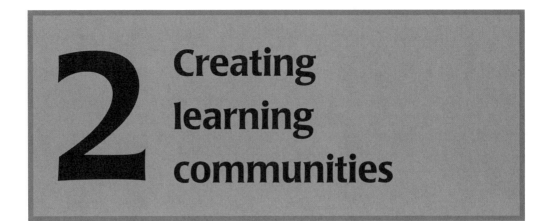

2 Creating learning communities

How do we create communities of learners? We design activities to get to know one another as learners and human beings. We create a classroom climate that honors differences and the open expression of differences. We welcome and encourage collaborative thinking and thoughtfully constructed collaborative-learning activities. In a genuine community of learning, we do whatever we can to ensure that all feel included and motivated to learn. Though we do assume leadership in our classrooms, in a genuine learning community everyone teaches and everyone learns.

Checking in/checking out

To generate student participation in small, discussion-based classes, I set aside five minutes at the beginning and end of class for "check-ins" and "check-outs." The technique works like this: Students sit in a circle, and I ask for one student to begin. We then proceed around the circle, with each person, including myself, responding to the question: "How are you doing?" I give no specifications nor place any constraints on the nature of our responses. Students may simply say, "I'm OK" (the response given most of the time); they may mention some problem they are having outside of class ("I've had a sick kid at home all week, and I'm really tired"); or they may bring up some course-related issue or problem ("I'm feeling angry about last week's discussion of pornography"). They understand that no one will respond to another's comment until everyone has been heard from. After that, anyone in the class may ask a question, offer sympathy, or make a suggestion in reply to another's comments.

Each time I have used this technique, the students and I have derived two major benefits. First, the students reported that it helped them become active participants in class discussions. For a minimum of two moments during every class period, each student must say something, and every other student must attend to her or him. Within a few weeks, they know each other's names and something about each other's lives outside of the classroom. The personalizing effects of the exercise, according to the students' own comments, helped them feel comfortable enough with each other to speak, to question, or to challenge. Second, on several occasions, it has helped me know when a particular topic or reading was creating difficulties for some students and enabled me to address the problem immediately or at the start of the next class period.

Obviously, the time involved makes this technique impractical for large classes or classes with short meeting times. I have used it in courses only with fewer than 20 students that meet once or twice a week for a minimum of 75 minutes. Under these conditions, it has proved an easy and fruitful way to begin and end each class meeting.

Judith DiIorio, Sociology and Anthropology, IPFW

Seriously seeking playful writing

Literary study is a communal enterprise. One of many effective ways to communicate this to students is for me to do the written work that I have assigned to them. Since I make a point of devoting a full class period to an analysis of student papers or excerpts, which I have typed and duplicated, I often conclude our reading and discussion of student work with a reading of my own essay or portions thereof.

I have had success with this practice: Students seem put at ease by knowing that I am performing the written work they have been required to complete, and they, consequently, come to view me as less an authority figure than as a fellow traveler in "the realms of gold," as Keats aptly described imaginative literature.

Yet such a practice is not always salutary. As a grader and critiquer, I suspect that my assessment of student papers can sometimes be skewed by the fact that I have defined through my own paper-writing what may emerge unwittingly for me as a paradigm for a successful critical essay. Just as problematic is the potential for students to become intimidated by what they may view as "competition" from their professor, despite the fact that many of their essays are truly outstanding and are often more effective, I feel, than mine.

To avoid such unintended consequences, I have come to limit my own written responses to assignments that are more playful than the usual critical essay yet no less central to the learning process. Such assignments have included 1) short rewrites, in conventional or straightforward prose, of the opening paragraphs of novels whose speakers are linguistically distinctive, quirky, complex, or opaque (for example, *Moby Dick*—"Hi, my name is Ishmael . . . ," *Heart of Darkness*, *Ulysses*); 2) an accurate, *but catchy*, dust-jacket blurb for a narrative whose strong emotional currents tend to lurk beneath a placid surface (e.g., *Emma*, *The Beast in the Jungle*, *The Dead*); 3) a poem in the style of the poet we are reading. (I've had most success with this assignment when teaching Walt Whitman; by creating our own "Whitman samplers," we all come to feel in our pulses the high artistry involved in Whitman's production of a singular, compelling voice through what appears to be a random listing of objects and sense impressions).

> **Students come to see me as less an authority figure than as a fellow traveler in 'the realms of gold.'**

Sharing our versions of openings to novels, of dust-jacket blurbs, or of poetic imitations and parodies works consistently well in sparking insightful discussion about what makes the texts we are reading so rich and inimitable. The fact that I have offered my own written contribution brings us together—playfully and seriously—as a community of readers and writers who have much to learn from one another and from the imaginative literature we are engaged with.

Lewis H. Miller, Jr., Honors Division and English, IU Bloomington

Revisiting the journal

Journals have long been used to foster informal, creative writing. However, I have found that journals can also provide a forum to develop formal analytical writing and encourage community, creativity, risk-taking, and interaction with textual materials.

Every two weeks I ask my upper-level rhetoric students to respond to course readings by applying concepts to the analysis of specific artifacts, or by creating discourse that relates to theories discussed in the readings. For example, in one of my courses I ask students to respond in their journals to a series of readings dealing with identity discourse of women of color. First they create their own identity discourse through prose, poetry, music, or the text of speech. Then they analyze the ways in which writing their own identity discourse facilitates connections, associations, and bridges to the discourse of marginalized people. It is not unusual for a white, 20-year-old male who initially rejected the readings as "angry, hostile, and overly aggressive," to reach heightened awareness and understanding after writing about his own "blue collar" roots and analyzing the connections between the two discourses.

The journals, as I use them, accomplish several other pedagogical goals. First, by

turning in rough drafts for many of their entries, students are able to work on and improve their writing and critical-thinking skills that have both general and course-specific applications.

Second, students meet in small groups throughout the semester to share journal ideas in a supportive, creative community where they learn from each other. I encourage students to take notes on each other and to cite each other in their journals. In this way students learn critical listening skills and also learn to value and appreciate the comments of their peers.

I also vary each of the journal-entry assignments to focus on different skills and to adapt to different learning styles of students. I assign brief literature reviews, think pieces, applications, and creative pieces.

Finally, the journal entries stimulate discussion by requiring students to be knowledgeable about the readings in order to complete the assignment. Journal entries also give them confidence in participating because they come to class with a written analysis about the discussion topic.

Final drafts of journals are collected twice during the semester; they typically number 25 to 30 pages, including extensive bibliographies and endnotes. I leave plenty of time to grade the journals, not only because grading is time-consuming, but because I enjoy charting the learning process for each student by comparing the earlier drafts to the final entries.

Every semester I am rewarded with feedback about how this assignment enhances students' abilities to formulate a critical set of questions and effectively analyze communicative acts, events, and artifacts.

Catherine A. Dobris, Communication Studies, IUPUI

It's her idea, not mine!

For some years, I had occasionally broken up my large lecture classes by giving students two or three minutes to discuss some emerging idea with a student sitting next to them. After they talked, I asked for volunteers to report on their results. I got a decent but not strong set of responses but continued the practice because I believed in the value of the discussion itself.

Things changed for the better when one day I asked for volunteers to report on the good ideas of the students sitting next to them. Three times as many hands went up, and the reports had a consistently better energy. I realized that I had solved a problem of "face" in a large class and have never looked back.

John A. Woodcock, English, IU Bloomington

Collaborative fieldwork

I have become very interested in involving students in both original fieldwork and collaborative learning, and I have been able to combine the two in a collaborative fieldwork project. Students collectively examine local examples of a broad problem such as inequality and joblessness in post-industrial economies (in my class on Social Stratification) or *de facto* community and school segregation (in my Race and Ethnic

27

Relations class). Each student compiles a brief annotated bibliography, a copy of which I put on reserve for common use. Then each conducts a visit and interview or a service project in a relevant field setting in the community such as a school, agency, major employer, or a neighborhood association. Students who have similar sites work together in small groups to develop questions and contacts. Each then writes a field report, which I also put on reserve, grouped with others from similar sites. Students also write "conclusion papers" assessing the local situation based on their fieldwork as well as on their reading of their classmates' reports.

Students enjoy learning more about their community through reading one another's accounts, and each has an added incentive to do quality work, knowing it will be read by everyone in the class. Formal in-class reports are not needed, but class discussions are enriched by students' community involvement and findings. The students continually interact with one another, both in class and on paper, but unlike a traditional group project, each is responsible for his or her own work and can be evaluated accordingly.

Scott Sernau, Sociology, IU South Bend

Case study in transparent teaching

One teaching strategy that has been extremely successful in my education courses is something I call "transparent teaching." In transparent teaching, I use my own teaching as a case study. I begin the first day by explaining the reasoning behind certain aspects of the syllabus, such as the timing of exams and the rationale for research papers. As the course continues, I often pause to reflect on some aspect of the teaching situation. For example, when I make a mistake (the activity "bombs" or the exam has some bad questions), I use it as an opportunity to discuss how teachers can learn from mistakes. When we cover motivation, I have the students analyze the various ways that they are motivated in the course and suggest strategies I could use to increase their motivation.

Recently, I adapted the transparent teaching strategy for a research class I developed for practicing K-12 teachers. As I discussed research approaches with the teachers, I reflected on how I was making research decisions for my own project, which examined how these teachers were learning to conduct research. We analyzed some of my research instruments and interview techniques, and brainstormed alternative research designs. At one point, I brought in my own reviewed manuscript, full of editing marks, to illustrate the peer-review and editing process. "Transparent teaching" had become "transparent research!"

Gwynn Mettetal, Education, IU South Bend

The autobiographical collage

If you can overcome your own and your students' suspicions of "arts and crafts" in the academy, the following can be a terrific ice-breaker. For classes that require students to learn the skills of interviewing, it can become the basis of a semester-long exercise in soliciting information from people you don't know, or at least do not know well.

Ask your students to gather up the following materials: a small piece of white poster board, old magazines, scissors, and glue. Instruct students to spend no more than 20 minutes tearing through old magazines to find images and words that tell something about who they are. Ask students to arrange the images and words into an autobiographical collage that takes up one half of the piece of poster board.

When they bring their collages to class, break students into pairs. Ask them to interview one another about the images so that they can introduce their partners to the class. After the introductions (often hilarious), use the exercise to talk about any number of issues that may be important to your discipline. In my discipline of journalism, we talk about sources and the selectivity of the information they present to journalists. We also talk about the selectivity of the information that journalists present to the public. We may talk, too, about using visuals to convey information (especially important for broadcast journalism), and about the kinds of images included in, and excluded from, magazine journalism.

> *It is enlightening for many of the students to learn that I am a multifaceted person—not just a walking head—as they are.*

When the introductions and discussion are over, I remind the students that the poster boards are only half full. I assign each class member the responsibility of finding, before the semester is over, one word or image to represent every other member of the class. To do this will require students to observe and interview one another (skills, in this case, that journalists need to cultivate). To make sure the students don't leave their information-gathering until the last minute, I frequently set aside 5 to 10 minutes during classes for students to pair up for short interviews.

On the final day of class, I bring in one paper lunch bag for each student. The students deposit their words or images in the appropriately labeled bags and then briefly share the words and images they have received.

The collage is the best ice-breaker I have ever used. At the end of one week, the sense of community in the class is as great as it typically is after three or four weeks. At the end of the semester, there is a sense of cohesion that is palpable. I do the assignments, too, and it is enlightening for many of the students to learn that I am a multifaceted person—not just a walking head—as they are.

S. Holly Stocking, Journalism, IU Bloomington

Just their type

Many teachers who use student groups in the classroom strive to diversify the groupings so multiple views can surface. Yet such a process can often prove lengthy, demanding more time than an already crowded syllabus permits. A technique I have used successfully is to group students based on similarities rather than differences, although this is counter to much of the literature on group dynamics. In ascertaining student similarities, I suggest using either the Myers-Briggs Type Indicator test, or for a quicker, less expensive and less time-consuming categorization, the Kiersey Temperament Test, which yields a briefer, less detailed version of the MBTI profile. The Kiersey test is available online on the World Wide Web and takes about 15 minutes to complete. (The URL is http://www.kiersey.com.) Similarities I have found most interesting are problem-solving preferences and temperament likenesses.

Creating groups of students with similar profiles usually means they will perceive a problem and its solution in generally the same way. Thus, student groups will come to closure far more quickly than if they were constituted more diversely. The advantage for the professor is that a classroom discussion can then be orchestrated in which groups present their often conflicting solutions. Thus, multiple views are aired at the group level and argued in the presence of all.

This method works quite well in case-oriented courses, but there is always a potential danger. The class may not contain the full array of group types (16 MBTI categories are possible), and the course discipline or major can also affect the number of group types. I once tested 16 students, and 13 were evaluated with the same profile (ISTJ—and for Myers-Briggs aficionados, this is not the most discussive of group types).

If you find the following . . .	be prepared to . . .
Too few group types:	abandon the group dialogue approach as it is unlikely to introduce the conflicting views you desire to explore.
I groups:	create a "jump start" to initiate discussion; the Introverted nature of this group makes initiating conversation sometimes difficult.
P groups:	keep the Perceptive types focused on concluding the task at hand; they tend to get sidetracked.
N groups:	hold the iNtuitives to a timetable for problem solution; they tend to explore too many options.

A more detailed discussion of this technique can be found in *Collaborative Learning*, 2nd edition, edited by Sharon Hamilton, 1997, published by the IUPUI Center for Teaching and Learning, Indiana University Purdue University, Indianapolis, Indiana.

Robert Orr, Computer Technology, IUPUI

Who am I?

Most students who enroll in my class on playwriting have only a limited understanding of how playwriting differs from other forms of writing—that a play is created for the stage, not the page. Many are shy and uncertain about their abilities to write dramatically, and they often know no one in class. The following exercise, which could be used in other subject areas, is fun. It develops a sense of community during the first class meeting, puts the students' writing into the hands of an "actor", and sets the tone for subsequent collaborative work. It also launches the student into writing in the opening moments of the class.

Before the students arrive, I arrange the seating in a circle. I also bring with me several items that don't look out of place, but which ensure that there are some interesting objects in the room. I can usually count on a wastebasket, clock, desk, and chairs, but some additional items, such as a coffee cup, my briefcase, a large rubber band, for example, sometimes add spice.

After introducing myself and asking members of the class to introduce themselves, I pass out a piece of lined theme paper. I ask the students to select an inanimate object in the room that is visible to all and to pretend that the object is alive—that it has a mind, a spirit, a voice. Then I ask them to write a monologue (first person) in which they reveal the perspective of that object without telling what it is. They have five minutes to produce at least a 50-word monologue. I write one also.

I collect these and pass them back to the students making certain that no one receives his or her own monologue. Then we read the one we receive silently to be sure we understand; at that point we become the "actors" and read them aloud. At the end we guess what the object is.

This shared experience releases a lot of creativity, helps students bond, and provides a springboard into understanding character and dramatic action. It also demonstrates that what we write provides the clues the actor uses in developing character. The following is an example.

> Pound, Pound, Pound!!! One more time and I'll scream—I can't take it any more. This sidewalk is hot, man! (pause) Chewing gum—oh God—chewing gum. Slow down. Pound, pound, pound—Ouch—the pressure is killing me. It'd help matters if you lost a little weight, you know! Only one more flight, then down the hall and through the door. Watch out for that chair leg. Oh-h—that was close. Stop flirting and find a seat. If you don't sit down soon, I'm going to have to hurt you. Oh-h—that's better. Now, before class starts, just lean over and loosen my tie a little.
>
> Who am I?
> (A shoe.)

Dorothy Webb, Communication Studies, IUPUI

Launching self-propelled people

The humanities offer optimum possibilities for developing the whole woman, the whole man. Most of our classes are relatively small. So the first and the last thing we ought to do is to learn as much as we can about each individual student. Ever since teaching my first class in 1938 (no misprint), my first assignment to students has been to give me a personalized, narrated, informal autobiography: where they come from, family, pets, hobbies, travels, schools, successes, hopes, friendships, disappointments, plans for college, for life. This is followed, within a week, by an appointment with each student, alone, for 20 or 30 minutes. (No, I don't "invite" them to come. All but a few won't. Pragmatic wisdom!) We just chat. I try to accentuate the relaxed nature of the conversation by the semi-living room ambience of my university study (easy chairs, carpet, paintings), and by sharing tea, coffee, soft drinks, and cookies. After a little while the students usually feel "at home" rather than exposed to the lion in his den. In the middle of the semester, everybody comes in for a second appointment so I (and they) can profit from our reciprocal reactions while the course is still in progress. Once a semester, we have the whole class over for an informal supper.

I have found these autobiographies, which I save, very helpful in reminding me what the "whole" student was like when they come, as so often happens, a year or two or three later asking for a recommendation letter. It is both pleasing and sad to hear them say, after so long an interval: "I am asking you to write because you are the only professor who ever really got to know me."

Ultimately, the greatest reward of teaching is the hope that your students will become your friends after all reciprocal obligations are over. I do not, however, favor the self-conscious "buddiness" in sloppy dressing, familiar name-calling, inappropriate external partying and other forms of favor seeking that are superficial substitutes for the real thing.

I have often told my students, on the last day of class, something like this:

"I hope you liked the course. I even hope you liked me. But what you think or feel now, under all this pressure, is far less important than whether our experience will help you to be motivated on your own, later on in life and work. Great things in life have been accomplished only by self-propelled people."

Henry H. H. Remak, Germanic Studies, IU Bloomington

Teach locally, learn globally

The courses I teach at the graduate level (sociology and anthropology of education, comparative education, education and social issues) attract students from diverse disciplines within and outside the School of Education; they also appeal to many international students. I consider all students as teaching resources and international students as particularly valuable but frequently overlooked aids in providing a global, richly contextualized dimension to the concepts I explore in my classes. Thus, I invite every international student on the first day of class to make a presentation, either individually or in a group, about the education system in his or her country. In this way, students who may be unaccustomed to, or shy about, talking in public in a foreign language are provided with a structured opportunity to make a significant contribution to internationalizing the content of instruction and expanding the horizons of students not familiar with other parts of the world. As the class proceeds, I encourage students to work collaboratively on one or two major writing assignments, such as take-home essay examinations or term papers, in order to reinforce my goal of having students from a variety of disciplines and cultures learn from one another and share different skills.

Robert F. Arnove, Education, IU Bloomington

Collaboration in large classes

I have struggled for several semesters to use small groups to encourage student collaboration and discussion in large classes, while trying to avoid some of the potential "pathologies" of group work. In mid-sized upper-level classes, occasional group response papers have worked very well. Students break into groups of five to discuss and answer a series of critical thinking questions or analyze tables, graphs, or quotes.

Collaboration is even more important in large introductory classes but has been more difficult to coordinate. Currently, I divide the students into groups of five (alphabetically for ease in recording grades). I have students bring a response page to class in which they ask a question or make a comment about the day's reading. During class (at the end of shorter classes or in the middle of long classes to provide variety in format), students break into their groups. I give them a page with four questions based on readings, lecture, video, or other class material. They record their answers on this page in the form of minutes from their group discussion. The group secretary rotates with each question to encourage all members to be involved. The page is graded on a four-point scale. All group members who turn in an individual response page get the group grade. Students who miss class or are behind in the reading can make up the points by doing the group questions on their own out of class. This accommodates unavoidable absences while encouraging in-class participation since it is easier to do this assignment as a group.

While groups meet, I read through the response pages and note questions to answer and points to clarify. When appropriate, groups report back to the whole class on their discussions. The various elements combine individual responsibility and group collaboration, and maximize discussion and interaction, yet my out-of-class grading is limited to the single-sheet group reports (10 for a class of 50). Once groups have coalesced, they can be used for other purposes as well, such as focus groups for evaluation, study groups for tests, and so forth.

Scott Sernau, Sociology, IU South Bend

Using a 'contract' on a commuter campus

To encourage students with multiple outside commitments to be prepared for class, I include a copy of a "contract" with my syllabus. Although I do not require the students literally to sign the contract, I do state that their remaining in the class after the contract is discussed signifies that they have accepted the contract. Here's a typical contract:

Students in this course must agree to the following:

1. Students will come to class prepared by having read the assigned material and having completed the written assignments at least 95% of the time.

2. Students will attend at least 95% of the class meetings.

3. Students will turn in materials on time.

4. Students will participate in computer conversations with other class members and/or the instructor as required.

5. Students will take tests on the assigned dates and will follow the instructor's policy regarding missing a test.

6. Students will contact the instructor during office hours, via computer or phone, if problems arise.

Almost all students reported being impressed that a professor was willing to put her side of the bargain into writing.

The instructor agrees to the following:

1. I will always be prepared with well-organized, meaningful material for every class meeting.

2. I will return written material within two class meetings after it is submitted.

3. I will return tests within two class meetings of the test date and will return petitions within two meetings of their submission.

33

4. I will maintain current records so that each student will know at any time his or her grade status.

5. I will participate in computer conversations with students.

6. I will provide, both by handout and by computer, details of written assignments and due dates at least one week before they will be used in class and/or at least one week before they are due.

7. I will maintain regular office hours and will arrange additional times for students as requested.

8. I will provide a very meaningful and productive learning experience for those students willing to do the work.

Students have reacted very positively to the contracts. Each semester, several students have reported that there were times when they prepared for class, when they would not have done so otherwise, because of the pressure of the contract. Interestingly, almost all students reported being impressed that a professor was willing to put her side of the bargain into writing. They respected my efforts which increased their respectful responses of being prepared for class.

Carol S. Steinhaus, School of Public and Environmental Affairs, IUPU Fort Wayne

First-day questions

Besides the usual first-day-of-class discussion of the syllabus, I give the students a brief summary of the topics we will be covering in the course. I then ask them to look over the syllabus and think of one question they would like to have answered during the semester. I explain that I return to these questions when discussing the course topics.

Students write the questions on index cards. I sort the questions by topic, and include them in my class notes on a particular topic. I try to incorporate the students' questions at appropriate times during the semester.

I use the questions as reminders of the issues that students feel are important and interesting. The questions help me show the class that I welcome student questions and that I want to encourage students' curiosity about the course material.

Barbara Fazio, Speech and Hearing Sciences, IU Bloomington

Learning students' names

Learning and using names can be very helpful in communicating personal interest to students and awareness of their participation. Unfortunately, it seems in larger classes I do not master names until the end of the semester. Having students make a name plate by tri-folding a sheet of paper (business letter style, but not tightly creasing the folds so it can stand up), and placing these on their desks or table helps. If desks or tables are in a circle or horseshoe, students can then begin to refer to one another by name in class discussion. For a still larger group where I cannot see all the desktops, I have had students turn in a "bio" page with a photocopy of a picture (such as their student ID) and something about themselves. I then review these when I need to, such as before class as students file in. I connect names and faces, and students receive the message that their participation is noted and recognized.

Scott Sernau, Sociology, IU South Bend

A piece of the learning puzzle

In elementary education methods classes, we encourage students to use creative methods once they become practicing teachers. We also stress the importance of planning lessons to meet the needs of the different kinds of learners. However, not often enough do we incorporate creative ideas into our own classroom instruction, and seldom do we plan for the various kinds of learners we encounter. This activity is an example of how one can take a boring lesson and create interest, heighten student involvement, address different learning styles, and, in general, increase student learning.

> **Seldom do we plan for the various kinds of learners we encounter.**

I take my lecture notes chronicling a sequence (say, the development of supervision in elementary education) and type them using a larger font (an 18-point size). I reproduce them on card stock and cut them up into several strips. The students, working in groups, are then instructed to put the strips together in what they think is the sequence of the development. After allowing ample time, I call on the first group to identify the first piece of the puzzle. In rotation, all the groups are called upon until all the pieces of the puzzle are in place. As a piece is properly placed or sequenced, I then lecture, amplifying on the fact listed on that puzzle piece.

This is an enjoyable activity that works, even with graduate students. It captures the attention of students and addresses the needs of both visual and auditory learners.

Vernon G. Smith, Education, IU Northwest

Socializing the classroom

Teaching the diverse student population of a smaller, urban commuter campus makes teaching both richly rewarding and challenging. Because I want active class discussion, shared ideas, and group interaction, I find it imperative to make the students who come from different backgrounds and locales comfortable with each other. So I spend some time in the first several weeks of class in what I call "socializing the classroom."

I tell the class about the importance of sharing ideas around the class. I ask students, one row at a time, to introduce themselves with first name only, hometown, year in school, and major. As they introduce themselves, I may interrupt with a comment about job opportunities in their field of study. If two are from the same town, I ask if they know each other, and then perhaps they can study together or at least compare results of an assignment. I ask if they are aware of campus services that may be of interest, such as the "Juggler's Network," an organization for returning adult students.

Repeated early in the course, this process rapidly breaks down barriers that may exist due to age, gender, race, or ethnic background. It certainly encourages free discussion among the students.

Robert B. Votaw, Geosciences, IU Northwest

35

From competition to community

Like everything that has potential for good, competition has its dark side. The competitive grade system is especially problematic for students just out of adolescence in a culture obsessed with competitive sports.

In the last 12 years, I have taught, by design, only freshman/sophomore courses in the Honors Division or equivalent seminars in the College of Arts and Sciences, limited to 15 to 20 students. They have lent themselves to unorthodox experimentation.

Written work. In these seminar-like courses, I give no tests or examinations at all. I assign essays, sometimes on the same topic for all, sometimes on a different topic for each student, sometimes on a topic chosen by each individually but approved as feasible by me. I return each essay with ample and specific comments plus a comprehensive assessment rather than a grade and a few random marginalia. In their essays, competitive motivation, showing their best, leads to mostly positive results. But some students feel programmed, externally or internally, to avoid exchanging ideas with other students as they think of the essay topic, because they do not want to be seen as dependent on other "competitors" or even because it might be construed as plagiarism. I tell them:

> Of course, you are free to discuss any aspect of your essay or any other relevant topic not only with me but with any other student. Your learning, your education comes as much from fellow students as from your teachers. In fact, nothing pleases me more than to hear that you are discussing some "hot" topic raised in class with friends outside of class; that is precisely what education should generate. The final essay is still yours. "The lion," as Paul Valéry has said, "consists of digested mutton." It will be a priceless lesson in how to absorb knowledge from all directions, accept some, reject some, and make the final result, for which you are responsible, your own. That's exactly what you will or should be doing throughout life.

Oral work. In students' oral work, almost paradoxically, the competitive pressure has not resulted in aggressive self-assertion but in silence to avoid disgrace before the whole class and the teacher. To offset this, I have . . .

1. divided the class into teams of approximately four students a week before the meeting when I expect them to report to their fellow students.

2. designated, for each team, a student chair responsible for arranging a private meeting of the team (without the teacher being present) prior to the reporting date in order to discuss the topic assigned to them. Communication among all students in the class is facilitated by a complete roster of all members of the seminar, with addresses and phone numbers, distributed in the second week of instruction.

When the day for the collective presentation arrives, the team chair . . .

1. presents the consensus of the group (if any), and/or outlines the disagreements, to the entire class;

2. then calls on individual team members to add or detract from any consensus;

3. calls for discussion among the panel members;

4. then acts as moderator for discussion with the entire class.

Before the class adjourns, I try to pull things together and add a final perspective.

During the entire event, I sit as far away as possible from the center of the action. As much as I like hearing myself talk—and I believe I am not alone in this—my most glorious moments in teaching have come when students forget that I exist and fight it out, intellectually, among themselves. I have found, to my delighted astonishment, that the same students who glance, not so furtively, at their watches when, in the heat of passionate discourse, I keep them overtime, stay for an additional 15 or 20 minutes without blinking an eyelid when their own crowd runs a good show. Added benefit: Through in-class student discussion they actually get to know each other, intellectually and socially. Student evaluations of instruction have consistently noted that benefit. Ultimate benefit: Much of America runs the same way—working committee, chair, consensus, demurrers, final summary, all but a vote.

Henry H. H. Remak, Germanic Studies, IU Bloomington

Exploring diversity through storytelling

Introducing students to the literature of diverse cultures is a somewhat risky task. The pitfalls are obvious. It is difficult to do justice to literary texts reflecting the beliefs and norms of a culture different from the American mainstream, particularly within the confines of a one-semester course. Armed with generalizations about cultural characteristics and differences, students tend to oversimplify the issues at the heart of cultural diversity, in effect, "domesticating" the unfamiliar, often unwittingly perpetuating cultural stereotypes. The teacher, moved to challenge shallow or "politically correct" readings, may come off as an ideologue. But, if superficial views of diversity remain unexamined, students may leave the class essentially unchanged, unwittingly perpetuating cultural stereotypes and, worse, unaware of their own attitudes.

This became very clear to me last spring when I taught for the first time a course in Native American literature. As we opened our class discussion the first evening, the students' comments revealed that they had very little factual information about Native Americans of today or yesterday. Rather, they had absorbed many vivid culturally and cinematically defined cultural concepts. Like many Americans, my students shared a kind of sentimental nostalgia for these "vanished" peoples and a wholesale indictment of white oppressors (again, familiar from the movies). When I asked the obvious question—did anyone claim Native American ancestry?—no one responded affirmatively. Clearly, they considered Native American history and literature romantic but remote, even in Indiana.

Discovering their connections through narrative subtly altered the way students responded to the assigned Native American literature.

This pervasive detachment threatened to deflect my goal of awakening an understanding of the Native American experience to provide a vantage point for reading imaginative literature. Thus, I hit on the idea of having students enter the experience through storytelling, in the spirit of Native American culture. Specifically, I suggested they pair off and exchange recollections of an experience in their own lives that in some

37

way involved Native Americans. When the students reported these back to the rest of the class, the results were illuminating. Not only did each student have a story to tell, but that story was far from a Hollywood representation, and characteristically, one that had never been shared with another person. Interestingly, despite their earlier disclaimers, over half of the students described an event involving a distant Native American relative. The students recognized, and wrote on their one-minute end-of-class papers, that studying this minority culture was not "purely academic."

The storytelling exercise clearly reminded students of how many cultural and personal attitudes they had absorbed and internalized. Moreover, discovering their connections through narrative also subtly altered the way students responded to the assigned Native American literature, allowed them to develop more complex and sophisticated cultural concepts, and enriched class discussion through its relationship to contemporary issues involving Native Americans (for example, the debate about establishing a Native American-run gambling casino in a nearby community). It's a strategy that I plan to adopt and use in other minority literature classes. As Native American storytellers themselves know, this practice closes the ideological and personal distance.

Eileen T. Bender, English, IU South Bend

A classy ice-breaker

To give hands-on experience with a number of the concepts I teach in my sociologically oriented education courses, I frequently will use the simulation game *Starpower*© the very first week of class. It is a wonderful ice-breaker for the class because it requires students to interact and negotiate—even hold hands—with one another, and it raises a number of ethical issues.

The game, which can be run in about 75 minutes, involves the formation of essentially a two-class society—a small group of elites and a large underclass; there is also a small middle class, which tends to disappear over time (does this sound familiar?). The elites eventually gain absolute power and usually become tyrannical, frequently provoking a revolt on the part of the underclass. There are many turns the game can take in illustrating how individual behavior is shaped by a social system, the nature of social mobility, social class identities and strategies for advancement, the nature of power in a society, and how social change may occur and with what consequences.

A debriefing either immediately after the game or at the beginning of the next class provides for a very stimulating discussion in which students begin to relate social science concepts and theories to their personal experiences with the game and with life. It is not uncommon for students to refer throughout the semester to their experiences in the game and how it illuminated the various social and educational issues we examined.

The game, *Starpower*©, copyright 1969 by R. Gary Shirts, is available from the Western Behavioral Sciences Institute, 1150 Silverado, La Jolla, CA 92037.

Robert Arnove, Education, IU Bloomington

Quick wits

While we teach, we learn.

Seneca

The art and science of asking questions is the source of knowledge. Any curriculum of a new education would, therefore, have to be centered around question-asking.

Neil Postman and Charles Weingartner

A teacher affects eternity; he can never tell where his influence ends.

Henry Adams

Teaching is the only performance art in which there are no rehearsals.

David Pace

The test of a good teacher is not how many questions he can ask his pupils that they will answer readily, but how many questions he inspires them to ask him which he finds hard to answer.

Alice Wellington Rollins

I never let my schooling interfere with my education.

Mark Twain

Tell me and I forget.
Show me and I remember.
Involve me and I understand.

Chinese proverb

To be a teacher in the right sense is to be a learner. I am not a teacher, only a fellow student.

Søren Kierkegaard

39

3 Fostering critical and creative thinking

When students learn to think, read, and write critically and creatively, they learn skills that will last a lot longer than the knowledge they acquire. What are some ways we can foster critical and creative thinking, reading, and writing? We can use traditional debates. We can use role-playing. We can create reading and writing assignments that challenge students' knowledge, beliefs, and expectations. We can even teach students (gasp!) to be New Yorkers.

How to be (gasp!) New Yorkers

Teachers know that discussion gives a chance for ideas to confront each other and cross-fertilize. But many of my students don't like argumentative discussion. It shuts them up because, as they responded on a questionnaire, they "don't like to be wrong."

In a Shakespeare class two years ago, I hit upon a strategy for fostering critical thinking. I told the students that Midwesterners are taught to be nice and not to confront others, but that I was going to teach them how to be New Yorkers, who like nothing better than a good argument.

I said that, as I reread *Romeo and Juliet*, I found myself agreeing with the interpretation of an old colleague, an interpretation that I had vigorously rejected 20 years before: "Romeo and Juliet are a couple of nice, but dumb, kids." I said I would lay out an argument on Tuesday to support the "dumb kids" interpretation, but that, on Thursday, the students would have to come up with at least one alternative interpretation.

Since the students knew I had not always felt that R&J were "nice but dumb kids," they need have no fear of offending me, and I promised not to report them to the Midwest Hospitality Board. On Thursday, the students developed two alternative interpretations, one seeing Romeo and Juliet as victims of a hostile world, and another seeing them as heroes for loving in a macho-violent society.

> *Students ought to play with an idea the way a cat plays with a mouse—which is to say, more than is needed just to catch it.*

The results supported my view that students ought to play with an idea the way a cat plays with a mouse—which is to say, more than is needed just to catch it. More precisely, students should not only develop a thesis and gather lots of evidence to support it, but they should also consider counter-evidence and alternative theses. The mere act of considering counter-evidence and alternatives to a cherished thesis often leads to new or more complex thinking.

For those who are interested, I have written a computer program called SEEN that leads students through this kind of thinking when engaged in literary analysis.

Helen J. Schwartz, English, IUPUI

Dig into primary sources

While the traditional library research paper certainly has its place as a teaching technique, I have found that students benefit greatly from anything that encourages original, primary-source research. This can begin to wean them from over-dependence on the analysis and ideas of others, and often gives me more interesting papers to read.

To this end I have found that a qualitative content analysis or textual analysis can be a good way to encourage students to draw on library resources in more original ways. My sociology students analyze gender stereotypes in the advertisements of contemporary magazines. They look at changing views of the family by examining the last several decades of *Life* and *Ladies Home Journal* (collecting dust in bound volumes at most libraries). They also can observe changing views of the world in volumes of *National*

41

Geographic that go back to the turn of the century, or compare ideals of gender relations and family life in *Esquire, Cosmopolitan, Mothering, Working Woman,* and *Family Circle.*

The comparisons of current publications encourage critical awareness that can be applied throughout students' lives. The historical studies offer a taste of original archival research, and they often amuse students, such as when they find a 1930s *Life* magazine describing the shock of topless bathing suits (for men), or describing Hitler as "a harmless eccentric." Finally, all of this work generates wonderful examples to contribute to class discussions.

Scott Sernau, Sociology, IU South Bend

Challenging students' beliefs

Students enter our classrooms with a variety of beliefs based on their own personal experiences. When teachers ignore these beliefs, students accept theories of "best practice" at a superficial level.

I have discovered through trial and error that I must challenge, and students must examine, their personal belief systems in ways that allow them to discover for themselves the biasing effects of their personal experiences. This is tricky, and success is never a sure thing.

Four activities that I have used to foster this process are the following:

1. I ask students to imagine themselves at their own retirement dinners and write what they would like to have others say about them in terms of the effectiveness of their career. From this they construct a personal vision statement for themselves and write two or three goals that they have for this particular class that will help them move towards this vision.

Using this activity as a baseline, several weeks later . . .

2. I ask students to consider their family experiences as a child. We discuss types of families; then we discuss how early family experiences have influenced them as parents or how they anticipate behaving as parents. We move this activity to the context of the classroom and to how their beliefs might influence their actions as teaching professionals. I then ask students to write their descriptions of the "perfect or ideal" student after two or three more weeks in which we have examined how and what affects classroom climate, communication as a tool for instruction, and discipline strategies that produce certain behaviors.

> *I ask students to imagine themselves at their own retirement dinners and write what they would like to have others say about them.*

3. I ask students to write their philosophy of education and particularly their philosophy of discipline and to compare that with their vision statement. What modifications are needed?

4. I then ask students to compare the philosophies they have constructed with their image of the perfect student they wrote previously to determine if their behavior and their actions as a teacher will produce their "ideal" student. If not, where do they need to make modifications—in the description or in their philosophy?

This is often the first time that students truly understand the relationship between their beliefs and their practice. It makes them examine theory through a more forward-looking lens.

Carol Browne, Education, IU East

What's new in the world today?

As a professor of political science, I often have students who neither read the newspaper daily nor closely follow political events in the world or in America. One of the goals of this daily but brief exercise—it takes no more than 10 minutes—is to encourage students to develop the habit of following political events or issues on a daily basis. Students begin to learn the who, what, when, and how of current world events. The exercise encourages them to participate in the class discussion. Perhaps most important, it serves as a tool to teach students how to apply concepts, theories, and abstract ideas to real world political phenomena.

Each class period I begin with the question, "What is new in the world (or America) today?" If I receive no response, which is normal on the first or second day of class, I talk about an article that I have read from the day's newspaper. I describe the thrust of the article and ask for comments. I select each article because it will allow me to make the transition into the major themes, concepts, ideas, or theories of the assigned readings. For example, discussing an article on Bosnia easily allows me to make the transition into the concepts of state, nation-state, and nation-building.

I continue this for the first three or four weeks of class. Students come to anticipate the question, and many begin to talk about articles before I prompt them with the question. After the third or fourth week of class, I begin assigning three or four students on a weekly basis to talk about recent articles in the newspaper. I emphasize that in addition to the who, what, why, when, and how of the article, they should explain how the article illustrates the major themes, concepts, ideas, or theories in the assigned readings.

One of the most common statements appearing on students' evaluations is that they now read the newspaper on a daily basis. As one student put it, "I now read the newspaper every day—something I had never done before." The most important goal, though, is for students to develop the ability to take what they have read in the newspapers or what they have seen or heard on other media and relate it to the major themes, concepts, ideas, or theories of the class.

Cliff Staten, Political Science, IU Southeast

Developing solid arguments

One of the goals for my senior seminar class is to help students organize the information they have acquired as psychology majors. In an effort to accomplish this, the students and I select 10 "hot" topics in psychology. These topics might include such items as the accuracy of repressed memories or whether watching violence on television leads to violent behavior. Once the topics are selected, articles addressing each issue are located and read. I select and locate the articles for the first two issues; after that, the students do it, in consultation with me. Care is taken so that the six to eight articles selected present both sides of the argument on the particular topic.

The first semester I used this approach I was greatly disappointed. Students came to class with their opinions but could not support their opinions with any evidence despite their reading of the articles. Frequently I would feel like I was in the middle of a bad *Saturday Night Live* sketch. The students would argue about an issue for 20 minutes only to have one student comment, "Well, those studies don't matter, I heard the opposite on a talk show." Pop quizzes on their readings did not seem to aid in this task.

For the past two semesters, I have attempted to solve these problems by giving the students a five-step process for class discussions. These steps include the following:

1. Define all terms. Don't assume all students begin at the same place.
2. Outline arguments on each side. At this point it doesn't matter how silly the arguments might be.
3. Present supporting evidence for arguments on each side: research studies, talk shows, etc.
4. Evaluate the evidence for arguments on each side. Yes, some evidence is better than others.
5. Reach a conclusion based on scientific merit. Usually the conclusion is complex, requiring several *caveats*.

> *No longer did [students] accept what the professor said at face value but would ask, 'Where's your evidence?'*

The first class period using this technique was arduous. The students had great difficulty defining the major terms (what is a repressed memory anyway?); they also had trouble proceeding one step at a time. By the third topic, though, the students had mastered the process and would correct the professor if she began to evaluate an argument while still in step three!

Not only did the students increase their ability to support their opinions with evidence, but they developed a sense of competency about their abilities and their knowledge of psychology. No longer did they accept what the professor said at face value but would ask, "Where's your evidence?"

Robin K. Morgan, Psychology, IU Southeast

Debating controversial issues

Citizens of democratic societies have preferred to cope with problems by thinking them through and submitting conclusions to an individual and/or group verdict. Debates provide opportunities for students to express their knowledge of controversial issues, to demonstrate their awareness of both sides of issues, and to render a rational stand for one side or the other.

I have found a variation to the formal debate format that stimulates student involvement in this strategy. After the affirmative and negative teams have presented their viewpoints and cross-examined each side, class members can ask questions or respond to the comments made by each team as it developed its positions.

Since few of my students have participated in a formal debate, I outline in the course syllabus the following debate format and the tasks and assignment of each debater:

A. Arrangement

1. First affirmative constructive speech, 4–6 minutes.
2. Cross-examination of the first affirmative by the negative rebuttals, 2–4 minutes.
3. First negative constructive speech, 4–6 minutes.
4. Cross-examination of the first negative by the affirmative rebuttal, 2–4 minutes.
5. Cross-examination of affirmative by class, 4–5 minutes.
6. Cross examination of negative by class, 4–5 minutes.
7. Negative rebuttal, 4 minutes.
8. Affirmative rebuttal, 4 minutes.

B. Suggestions for Debaters

1. Conduct research for the debate.
   a. adopt a plan of procedure.
   b. acquire a general background.
2. Assemble supplementary materials.
3. Record and arrange notes for effective use.
4. Plan ahead for rebuttal and refutation; anticipate your opponent's attack.
5. Outline your argument and the anticipated argument of your opponent. The burden of proof resides with the anticipated argument of your opponent.

C. Duties of the Affirmative

1. Define the terms in the proposition.
2. Establish a need for the proposition.
3. Show how the proposition is superior to the alternative proposition.

D. Duties of the Negative

1. Respond to the interpretation and analysis of the affirmative in rebuttal or rejoinder by:
   a. denying the affirmative's proposition.
   b. supporting the alternative proposition.
   c. supporting the negative proposition with revision.

E. Specific Duties of Affirmative and Negative Speakers

1. First Affirmative Speaker
   a. have a set speech.
   b. state the proposition and define terms that might need clarification.
   c. state the position of the affirmative team.
   d. summarize.
2. Cross-Examiners
   a. confine speaking to questioning the evidence, statements, or reasoning of the opponent, but not to interpreting or evaluating the comments of the opponent.
   b. expect an answer for a question, not filibustering or avoiding the question.
3. First Negative Speaker
   a. refute the affirmative case based upon the case of the first affirmative speaker and upon information gleaned from the cross-examination.
   b. do not miss the specific case brought to bear by the first affirmative speaker.

        c. introduce the negative's proposition.
    4. Negative Rebuttal
        a. review the case of the affirmative and show its weaknesses.
        b. close the case of the negative.
    5. Affirmative Rebuttal
        a. present the main issue of the affirmative.
        b. close the case of the affirmative.

The debate strategy stimulates critical skills on the part of the participants, and it is an excellent way to get the entire class involved in studying controversial issues.

John C. Moody, Education, IU Southeast

Organized chaos in the classroom

I am always eager to create a classroom environment that emphasizes active participation. By active, I mean a situation where students are not just sitting there writing down what they hear, but rather are actively engaged in analyzing, evaluating, and synthesizing the materials. I have found that you can predispose students to those sorts of conceptual activities by visiting organized chaos upon them, and I do just that quite frequently.

Today in class I will say something, maybe just a sentence or two, that does not seem to fit reasonably into the topic we are covering. Two weeks from now I'll bring it up again, in a different context, perhaps with an humorous statement about how it wasn't irrelevant after all. After I've done this a few times, students find themselves on the alert whenever I say anything that seems strange. They start reviewing the ideas and materials we have covered. They start anticipating what I might be aiming at in future lectures. They start making associations. In short, an atmosphere of critical analysis is established through the back door, via an apparent guerrilla approach to teaching. I am careful to let students know I know what I'm doing, lest they let themselves off the hook by assuming I'm just not a good teacher.

> *An atmosphere of critical analysis is established through the back door, via an apparent guerrilla approach to teaching.*

Another way I do the same thing is by responding to students' questions as opportunities to infuse large doses of new material into the discussion, much of which will harken back to previous class hours, and much of which will just hover there, waiting to be plugged into future topics and issues. I point out that I have answered the question "extensively," or used it as a springboard to consider a collection of other ideas. And I drop little hints, sometimes (after students get to know my style) just by raising my eyebrows, that there is more to this than might instantly be apparent.

Yet another form of organized chaos comes from telling stories. Let's say I'm making a point about the ways the spirit of adventure and entrepreneurship in Africa influences art. I might then say I want to tell a story about the legendary founding of an ancient trade town. All kinds of tidbits will be in that story, tidbits that later can be connected like the slippery arms of an octopus to numerous other central issues of discussion. And each time that happens, I can remind the students of that story I told five weeks before

and then dive into its relevance for the moment. The original story may have taken seven minutes to tell, and lots of what I said could surely have been construed as fluff when held up against the subject then under discussion. But here too, after I have done it a few times, students are primed to think while listening, and they start making very useful and worthwhile connections, even without further prodding from me.

Patrick McNaughton, Art History, IU Bloomington

Is it just me, or is that guy crazy?
Using role-playing to show the importance of observational skills

Students usually enter psychology courses with the impression that disorders are both easy to identify from their symptoms and readily classified. To demonstrate both the difficulty of classifying behavioral symptoms and the importance of developing good observational skills as a psychologist, we use a role-playing demonstration.

One week prior to our discussion of psychological disorders in the general psychology course, we ask for a volunteer to be trained to help us with a demonstration. In private, this student volunteer is given a complete description of "Borderline Personality Disorder" and coached in ways to illustrate relevant symptoms behaviorally. This student then agrees to illustrate such behaviors at the beginning of the class period directly following our in-class discussion of psychological disorders.

During the demonstration class period students are randomly assigned to "diagnostic groups of three to five persons." Students are informed that their job is to objectively observe the subject's behaviors and to objectively record only what they are observing. After the student volunteer has completed his or her display, each student in the diagnostic groups is asked to write down three questions that he or she feels would be most critical for a clinician to ask in order to accurately diagnose the illustrated disorder.

Once the students have completed these tasks (objective observation, objective recording, and critical question-generation), members of each diagnostic group are asked to compare notes. Several key concepts can be illustrated during this comparison including: 1) any errors in the descriptions, 2) any assumptions made within the descriptions (such as statements like "she aggressively kicked the chair"), and 3) differences among the descriptions of individuals within each diagnostic group.

After this comparison period, each group is asked to share at least one question that they would like to ask a clinician about the displayed disorder. Again, several concepts can be illustrated with this question-session, including: 1) how questions might be biased by assumptions made within the descriptions, 2) differences in what students feel are the important questions to ask, and 3) how students might ask more objective (or non-biased) questions.

This entire demonstration is followed by a discussion on the importance of objective observation in the diagnostic process, and we give guidance on the challenges that face clinicians as they attempt to decipher observed behaviors and reach objective conclusions.

We do not have students speculate on what disorder was being displayed because we do not want to reinforce the opinion that diagnosis is quick and easy. In addition, we require students to write a short reflection paper addressing what they have learned.

Randall Osborne and Tim Basford, Psychology, IU East

47

Questions for critical reading and discussion

One of the challenges of generating active discussion in the classroom is the difficulty students have in comprehending the demanding material they read. To facilitate their understanding, I prepare discussion questions to accompany each reading. These discussion questions are designed to help students 1) identify the central point of each reading assignment, 2) create illustrations of key concepts and theoretical perspectives (often from their own experiences), and 3) critically assess the strengths and weaknesses of the assigned reading. We then use these questions as a starting point for our in-class discussion of the material.

Students often come to class unsure of how to respond to some of the questions. As the instructor, I refuse to provide the "correct" answer but make the students work through the questions in group discussion. For some students this strategy is quite frustrating. However, the students often find that questions that baffled some of them were well-understood by others; on other questions, the roles may well be reversed. In this manner students take turns teaching one another. Having to explain the material to another student facilitates understanding and learning for the "teacher" as well as the "student."

Jay Howard, Sociology, IUPU Columbus

Create a poem, a skit, a song . . .

When students can apply or use the knowledge they have mastered, they have achieved the highest level of learning. I have devised a few creative activities that both facilitate this level of learning and bring students together for an enjoyable interaction. After a lecture or presentation, I divide the class into groups and instruct them to use some of the information they have acquired to do one of the following creative activities:

> *When students can apply or use the knowledge they have mastered, they have achieved the highest level of learning.*

1. develop a skit
2. compose a song
3. write a poem
4. organize a debate
5. compose a rap
6. write a short story
7. create a poster or illustration

I allow the groups approximately 10 minutes. After completing the task, they share their work with the class. Below are examples of work that groups produced after a lecture on learning styles.

Example A
Types of Learners
I—is for ideas
People with imagination
Who relate well with self
And have high determination

Example B
I Believe I Can Fly
If you let me tell a story
I learn linguistically,
If you let me solve a problem
I learn logically—mathematically

48

A—is for analyzers
Who enjoy knowing all the facts,
Clear, concise explanations
To attack the task

P—is for pragmatist
A do-er who wants to know/
   how things work;
He thinks taking notes
Boy, that's for jerks

S—is for self-discoverers
Who want to solve all problems;
They are curious as a cat
And like experimenting using a rat

If you let me draw a picture
I learn spatially,
If you let me sing a song
I learn musically

If you let me move around
I learn kinesthetically,
If you let me lead
I learn interpersonally

If you let me work independently
I learn intrapersonally,
If you let me see
I learn visually
If you let me listen
I learn auditorially,
If you let me do all these things
I know I can fly

Vernon G. Smith, Education, IU Northwest

A question of understanding

How many times have you paused after making some point during a lecture and asked, "Did you all understand that?" Rarely does that question, which I too often ask in my own classes, elicit any response. How do you know if you don't understand something? How do you know if you do understand something?

One way to know is being able to do something with the information. I used to ask students questions to respond to orally, but this was ineffective in my large lecture class. Most students sat back, waited for someone to answer the question, and seemed to pay little attention to the answer. Now, I pause periodically after trying to explain a concept and say, "Now if you understand what I have just been going over, you should be able to answer this question."

I have the question on an overhead in a form that the students will see on the exam. I ask how many people are unsure of the correct answer. Depending upon how the students respond, I do one of several things: 1) Frequently I do not answer the question; I tell them to ask me about the question at the next lecture. 2) I sometimes use the question to start the next lecture. 3) In an introductory class, I occasionally try to model how to answer a multiple-choice question by considering and rejecting the various alternatives. 4) I also tell the students that I will go over the questions that we haven't answered in class at an evening review session.

Although any type of question could be used in this format, I generally use those that require the students to apply what they have learned. For example, after presenting several theories of pitch perception, I describe an experiment and the results from that experiment. The question can then be framed as: "Which theory do these data tend to support?" One can go on to ask how Theory A might have to be modified to take account

49

of these data, or a favorite question of mine: "What would the results of such an experiment have to be for the results to support Theory A?" In addition to teaching about pitch perception, I hope that questions such as these will help students see how theories need to be modified or rejected on the basis of new data and that there may be few, final right answers.

> **I generally use those [questions] that require the students to apply what they have learned.**

The extent to which presenting questions in this way is successful depends in part on constructing questions that cover key points in the course and in part on causing students to be slightly uncomfortable if they are unsure of the correct answer. To make it clear that it is worthwhile to understand the questions that I have presented in class, I include several of these questions, or variations of them, on sample questions that I give out before the exam and on the exam as well.

James Craig, Psychology, IU Bloomington

Don't confuse the model with reality

In the introductory course in American politics, I introduce students to different models of the political system. I explain that these models represent different views about how the political system works. I also explain that, while models serve the purpose of aiding our understanding about how the system works, they are not the same thing as the system itself. Yet, students often treat these models as if they are the real world rather than the representation of it.

To help students see the difference, I show them René Magritte's drawing of a pipe, which has written in French beneath it, *"Ceci n'est pas une pipe."* (This is not a pipe.)

I ask the class to discuss what they think Magritte might have been trying to say. Ultimately what I want them to see is that the illustration is a drawing of a pipe, and not a real pipe—that is, it cannot be lit, it cannot be smoked, etc.

Then I explain that, in the same way that the drawing of a pipe is not a real pipe, a model of the political system is not the same as the political system. Since it is not and cannot be an exact replication of the political system, it therefore distorts the real world.

The purpose of the exercise is to teach students that models serve heuristic purposes, helping us to see and understand things with more clarity. Models can be evaluated in terms of the extent to which they achieve these objectives. If a model is too out of touch with the real world, then it is less useful to us. However, used with the proper perspective, models are helpful tools for analyzing and directing inquiry about the world of politics.

Linda Gugin, Political Science, IU Southeast

Research projects and job skills

In my upper-level sociology courses, I require students to write a research paper on a topic of their choice. Papers are due a month prior to the end of the semester. I grade and extensively comment on the papers. Students then have the option of accepting the grade they earned or rewriting the paper for a higher grade. Students also present their findings to the class and field questions from their classmates about the paper in a manner similar to a professional research conference.

Students often complain that this is an especially time-consuming and difficult project. To help them see its value, I point out that it builds the very skills that local employers want most in their employees. A recent survey of large and small employers in the area identified the following 10 most desired skills for entry-, middle-, and top-level positions:

1. basic math skills
2. listening skills
3. verbal skills
4. time-management skills
5. reasoning skills
6. flexibility
7. basic English skills
8. writing skills
9. problem-solving skills
10. people skills

I point out that, if a student collects and analyzes data for the paper, basic math skills are used. In the writing of the paper, reasoning, problem-solving, time-management, writing, and basic English skills are all used and developed. In the presentation of the results and fielding of questions, verbal skills and flexibility are developed. In the revision process, students have an opportunity to improve their reasoning, writing, English, problem-solving, and time-management skills, and they learn major concepts in sociology as well. Students often find this, admittedly pragmatic, rationale sufficient to encourage them to tackle the project with less grumbling and more determination.

> **Students have the option of accepting the grade they earned or rewriting the paper for a higher grade.**

I tell students I will reward those who write the best papers with an opportunity to present the paper at the Midwest Student Sociology Conference, an undergraduate conference. I remind them that such presentations also look very impressive to an employer who is scanning a resume! The end result is that a number of students look at their research projects in a new light and with new motivation.

Jay Howard, Sociology, IUPU Columbus

Teaching language through literature

In the last five years administrators in many American universities have increasingly sought to reduce, and almost suppress, the teaching of literature in foreign language programs. Why? It is said that students need foreign language to communicate effectively and that literature is not conducive to this goal. More practical courses, it is said, should be substituted for literature courses. Students, contaminated by a general prejudice against the humanities, arrive in literature classes with a skeptical look: "What am I *really* going to learn in this class?" The question then is: How to teach literature to foster and increase the four basic skills in foreign language acquisition—oral comprehension, oral communication, written communication, and reading?

In the last four years, I have consistently found that the literature courses I am teaching are by far the favorite of my students, much more than other supposedly more "practical" courses. In the comments of my course evaluations, students repeat how much they have learned and enjoyed the class. To quote one: "We had so much fun in this class, and the beauty of it is that I continue to learn more and more."

Here is what I do. Every day students are assigned a literary short story to read at home. After reading it, students have to answer a questionnaire and discuss, in a longer paragraph, the meaning of the story, and why or why not they can identify with the characters or with the conflicts in the story. This written homework has to be turned in on my desk before starting each class; otherwise they lose the homework points. At the beginning of the class, the students have 10 minutes to discuss in small groups their own ideas about the story, without their written comments. Meanwhile, I go from group to group to supervise their discussion. After this period, we start the class discussion guided by my questions. I also lecture for about seven minutes at the beginning, as an introduction, and for five more minutes at the end, to summarize the main conclusions. (The class lasts one hour and 15 minutes.) The students are required to take written notes while I am lecturing. All the reading, writing, and speaking is, of course, in Spanish.

After all this process, what is accomplished is much more than understanding a literary piece within its cultural context. Before each class period, the students have already accomplished the following: 1) reading, 2) writing, and 3) developing their critical and creative thinking by reflecting on the meaning of the story and expressing their reactions. In class, the focus is: 1) speaking, 2) listening, and 3) taking notes in Spanish, but also 4) continuing to develop their critical thinking abilities, and 5) creating learning communities by getting to know one another and by collaborating in small group discussions. By the end of the semester, the bonds among the students are strong, and they feel they have accomplished many goals.

I also learn from my students. Through their written work and class discussions, my own notes on the stories always grow.

Margarita Lliteras, Spanish, IU Southeast

Issue papers: Short and to the point

Over time I have assigned my students of school law various research/writing projects, ranging from in-depth research papers to annotated bibliographies. However, I always was searching for an assignment that would be more meaningful to the students. Finally, I hit upon a strategy that seems to challenge students and assist them in cultivating their research and writing skills.

The assignment is to select an issue where the law is *not* clearly settled (for example, student-initiated prayers during public school graduation ceremonies). The student chooses a position to argue (for example, allowing students to decide whether to have student-initiated graduation prayers violates the Establishment Clause of the First Amendment). Papers are evaluated on how well the position is argued, *not* on the position selected. I provide a list of potential issues, but students also have the option of selecting other topics. They must check their topics with me so I can steer them away from issues that are not controversial or where resources are scarce.

Students are instructed to develop arguments to support their positions in four pages or less. Students in this course primarily aspire to be practicing administrators, and as such, they will not have the luxury of writing 20 pages to develop the points they wish to get across to their constituencies. Requiring these papers to be short forces students to weigh their words. I indicate that I expect them to start with a lot of notes and to write several drafts until they have condensed their major arguments into four pages. This forces them to write concisely, and it eliminates material not essential to their arguments.

> *Students have found that shorter papers not only can be better, but also can be harder to write because of the numerous revisions necessary.*

Part of this activity entails students becoming familiar with legal research strategies. They are to provide legal support for any generalizations or conclusions in their papers and to give some attention to counter-arguments and to why such arguments are not persuasive. I also strongly encourage students to have classmates, spouses, and friends review their papers and suggest improvements. This pattern of sharing written work and soliciting suggestions is one I hope the students will adopt when they are called on to do professional writing. In addition to my extensive feedback, I usually divide the students into groups to discuss their topics; this works particularly well when several students have selected the same topic.

I have found these papers to be far tighter than papers I previously assigned with no page limits. The latter often contained a lot of filler, as if a longer paper was automatically better. Students have found that shorter papers not only can be better, but also can be harder to write because of the numerous revisions necessary to condense the important points. While students find this assignment difficult, they also indicate that it challenges them and motivates them to improve their research and writing skills. Often in their jobs, they will be called on to justify their position or argue a point of view, and this assignment provides good practice.

Martha McCarthy, Education, IU Bloomington

Professional journal scan

Getting students to turn to professional journals as a means of enhancing their professional preparation is not an easy task. I recently gambled on a way to achieve this and hit the jackpot. I incorporated a "journal scan" into one of my class sessions for secondary education English Methods students. It was as simple as 1, 2, 3.

1. I assigned every student in the class a month and year. They were instructed to meet at the library at the beginning of the next class session and scan both the *English Journal* and the *Journal of Adolescent and Adult Literacy* for their respective month and year. They were to make notes on each journal's content, format, and articles that particularly caught their attention. Students were then to reconvene as a group and be prepared to share their findings during the second hour of the class.

2. At the beginning of the next class session, students worked independently on the actual journal scan. They spent approximately 30 minutes scanning each journal.

3. During the second hour of class, I joined the students in the library where we met as a large group. Students decided to share their findings in chronological order by month and year, starting with earlier editions and progressing to current issues. One at a time they shared observations about the *English Journal* and the natural comparisons and contrasts to the *Journal of Adolescent and Adult Literacy*. For example, students began to notice that *English Journal* is thematic while *Journal of Adolescent and Adult Literacy* relies too heavily on topical columns that appear in every issue.

The students immediately expressed their satisfaction with this assignment. Since they all have "expert" presentations to do at a subsequent class meeting, this helped them locate which journal issues contained information relevant to their topics. They admitted that they "got hooked" on particular articles while they scanned and had to stop and read. Several students have since joined the professional organizations responsible for the publications.

Kevin Sue Bailey, Education, IU Southeast

Finding poetry

To overcome students' resistance to poetry as a genre, I often begin our study of poetry by asking my students to write a brief essay on a "found" poem.

> I'd like you to "find" a poem or to think of a time in the past when you encountered a poem within a specific physical or emotional context. The "poem" need not be a traditional poem; it might be culled from a cook-book, a wall, a phone message, a song, an advertisement, etc. Begin your paper by quoting the poem, and then proceed to explain just how the cir-cumstances (time, place) surrounding your finding and reading of the poem influenced your response to it.

The following student response (by Abby Rose) offers, I feel, a piquant lesson about poetry's ubiquity and about its public and private, objective and subjective modes of appeal and interpretation:

> *Bethesda, Friendship Heights, Tenleytown*
> *Vaness-UDC, Cleveland Park, Woodly Park and the Zoo*
> *Dupont Circle, Farragut North, Metro Center*
> *Gallery Place, Judiciary Square, Union Station.*

> A dozen stops in the midst of the Washington, DC metro area transit authority's red line make up my found "poem." These names are engrained in me, like the essentials of speech, from earliest childhood memory. They represent my independent youth: pre-car, pre-fear, pre-existence. An urban gamine, I was loose within the bounds of those twelve subway stops which made up my world.

> As an older child, a high school graduate, riding the train alone and scared, I looked at the succession of names, these old friends, with new appreciation. I'd never before, in the countless jaunts, zooming back and

54

forth in the cool repose beneath my hometown streets, really listened to the words. Gallery Place . . . Judiciary Square . . . there's a definite, accidentally musical cadence and alliterative flow of syllables. I said each one alone and in its proper order, paying careful attention to each delicious sound.

Then, a small freshman, shocked at both the smallness and largeness of Bloomington, five hundred miles away from the only home I'd ever known, I was miserable. Many times, face buried in a tear-soaked dormitory pillow, I'd recite my "poem," over and over again like a mantra, in groups of three. And I would be calm, and I would fall asleep comforted.

What transformed these dots on a metro map from the ordinary into the meaningful, and even poetic? The richness and sounds of the very words may be enough, but also the concreteness of what they represent is important. People grow and change, but stone and metal and the names of places rarely do. When I visit DC, where I haven't lived for close to four years, I can click back into my old subway routine with the familiarity of an everyday best friend.

But it's more than "cheesy" nostalgia, really, these are wonderful names. A five mile, upscale, elite area which is the border between DC and Maryland has been dubbed "Friendship Heights." I've often pondered the irony of this title. Judiciary Square is literally the location of the court house, the mayor's office, and my mother's office in the U. S. Department of Labor building. One day, I was walking there with my mom when we saw a street person, apparently lying dead at the foot of one of our capital's prettiest memorial statues. Lawyers and government flunkies and other city denizens alike simply stepped over his stiffened limbs with as much regard as if he were a pigeon lying there, and not a man. Where is the justice in that?

So I guess the final element which makes this "poem" special to me are my personal experiences and history within each name and place. I have no idea who Tenley may have been, or how he came to have a town named for him, but Tenleytown is the stop where the Washington School of the Ballet is, where I spent the lion's share of my teenage years. And of course there's Bethesda, the most welcome name of all: a savior like its Biblical namesake because that was the end of the line for me, my home station.

Lewis H. Miller, Jr., Honors Division and English, IU Bloomington

Helping students understand ADD

Students in psychology courses often find it difficult to truly understand the impact of the psychological problems that we discuss. This seems to be especially true of cognitive problems such as Attention Deficit Disorder. Building on the idea of "give a student a disorder" that we have witnessed in many other classes, we decided to provide students with a behavior that would severely limit their capabilities. Unlike a physical limitation such as blindfolding them, however, we needed to develop a strategy that would duplicate some of the cognitive challenges associated with Attention Deficit Disorder.

Students drew numbers from a basket and were assigned a behavior based on that number. For example, those drawing number one were told to tap the pointer finger on their nondominant hand the entire time that they were trying to write down a page of information from the overhead screen. Students who drew number two were told to count to five, glance out the window, look back, count to five, glance out the window, etc. at the same time that they were expected to write down that same page of information. Others were sent out into the hallway for about one-half of the exercise (it seems that their behaviors had caused the teacher to label them as disruptive) and then were asked to start with the last sentence and write from the bottom of the page to the top, and some were told that they had no disorder.

At the end of the five-minute time period, students were asked to count the number of words they had managed to write down, and the mean score for each group was calculated. Needless to say, few of the students were very successful in their efforts to write down the required information. A lively discussion followed this demonstration. In addition to demonstrating many of the cognitive deficits associated with Attention Deficit Disorder, we were able to focus discussion on classroom design and how it may actually exacerbate the very problems that we hope to avoid.

After this demonstration and the subsequent discussion of ADD and other disorders resulting in cognitive challenges, students were asked to write a reflection paper imagining that they were a teacher. Their goal was to create a classroom environment that did not use these challenges against the student.

After the students turned in their completed reflection papers, small groups were formed and students discussed their ideas.

In the past we asked one of our adult students with Attention Deficit Disorder to come to this class period and discuss the suggested strategies for making the classroom more conducive for his or her learning. Feedback on this entire demonstration and especially the follow-up discussion with the adult learner with ADD has been very positive.

Randall E. Osborne and Joe Norman, Psychology, IU East

Quick wits

It's not what is poured into a student that counts, but what is planted.

Linda Conway

The task of the excellent teacher is to stimulate "apparently ordinary" people to unusual effort. The tough problem is not in identifying winners. It is in making winners out of ordinary people.

Pat Cross

Teaching is the highest form of understanding.

Aristotle

Thought flows in terms of stories—stories about events, stories about people, and stories about intentions and achievements. The best teachers are the best storytellers. We learn in the form of stories.

Frank Smith

Professors known as outstanding lecturers do two things: They use a simple plan and many examples.

Wilbert J. McKeachie

The educator must above all understand how to wait, to reckon all effects in the light of the future, not of the present.

Ellen Key

Every truth has four corners: As a teacher I give you one corner, and it is for you to find the other three.

Confucius

Human history becomes more and more a race between education and catastrophe.

H. G. Wells

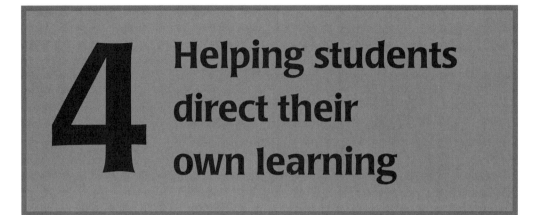

4 Helping students direct their own learning

Learning, even in the classrooms of the most gifted teachers, can be hard. In a college or university setting, particularly for beginning students or students who have not come well-prepared, it can be downright daunting. How can we best support our students to rise to the challenges? We can help them to think about what makes a successful student. We can help them to understand the difference between an argument and a discussion. We can create activities that encourage them to take charge of their own learning. In all these ways, and more, we can teach about learning and help students take responsibility for what they do and do not learn.

The five habits of successful students

I wanted to make the freshmen in a large lecture class think about which behaviors would be productive over the course of the semester and which would limit their success. Therefore, in the second class period, I divided the students into small groups and asked each to generate "five habits of successful students," borrowing an idea from a popular self-help book but reducing the number of items to a more manageable size. I then paired teams and asked them to reduce their combined lists to five items. By repeating the process, I ended up with four or five lists that I then placed on the board. As a final step, the class as a whole had to choose which items to drop as I progressively narrowed the list to 10 items. At the end of the process, I had a list of rather well-chosen patterns of behavior that really could contribute greatly to success in college and which students themselves owned.

David Pace, History, IU Bloomington

The toughest test of all

Although I long have included student questions in my exams, one semester I had the class create the entire final for themselves. I hoped to use the very process of constructing the exam as a way of encouraging students to think about the course and see the relevance of the readings to their own worlds. I also hoped to complicate and enrich teacher-student interaction by having students see themselves in both roles for a time.

For the last session of class, I asked students to come prepared with questions from which we would build the final. We began by putting all the questions on the board and then talked about which ones to include, a discussion that turned into a review of the major themes and concepts of the course. Although there were some traditional English questions on nature symbolism and interpretation of key quotes, most of the students asked questions that directly or indirectly related the readings to their own experience. They asked about how characters escaped the pain of love and about how problems of adolescence and growing up are reflected in society today. They wanted to talk about which work they liked most or least, and why.

The resulting exam was different but by no means easier than the more conventional one I had devised. Difficulty, in fact, was the first objection I got to the whole process ("I'd rather just sit down and answer the questions you give us"). As we got into it, however, most of the students became caught up in the process of creating exam questions and discussing what makes a good question—good,

> *Most of the students asked questions that related the readings to their own experience.*

that is, in terms of posing a real problem and in terms of giving them something to say. Students learned to distinguish between short-answer and long-answer questions. They learned that the way a question is posed can help one to respond. Wording also became an issue, which turned into a brief exercise on style, as we tried out different versions of each question.

The final exam the students wrote (it was done in class) was generally the best work they did that semester. They wrote more detailed answers, and one could sense the com-

59

mitment to the questions they had chosen. I was also impressed by the length of their responses, many of them writing up to 10 pages, where in the midterm they had done only three to five pages.

Comments in the student evaluations supported my sense that this was a successful experiment, although two students still felt that it was too difficult ("Proved how difficult an exam can be to write, but I would have preferred not to make it," and "I thought that it was a good idea for the final, but it was difficult to generate questions").

Nine out of the remaining 11 responses, however, were fully positive. Several students said that they appreciated the chance to create their own questions and write about something they enjoyed ("It is an opportunity I've never had").

But, of course, my favorite comments are those that express exactly what was the purpose of the exercise in the first place: "I liked the fact that we made up questions for our own exam because it forced us to think about what was relevant and what were the important things we read and talked about in class throughout the semester," and "It makes me have to really think about the material in advance, where in a regular essay exam I wouldn't."

Gabrielle Robinson, English, IU South Bend

Learning from exam results

Many instructors have had the unpleasant experience of an entire class performing poorly on an exam. When this occurs, instructors may worry that there was a problem with the exam or wonder whether students used appropriate study strategies. Additionally, students who perform poorly often become defensive and frustrated, creating a classroom atmosphere that is not conducive to learning.

To acquire information about students' perceptions of an exam, encourage them to think critically about their test performance and study habits, and diffuse feelings of frustration, we employ a one-page survey. Below is a list of questions we often include. While we do not ask all these questions every time, preferring to tailor the survey to the course, we encourage inclusion of the last three questions. These questions encourage students to take personal responsibility for their performance and let students know you are willing to help. Students complete the surveys after they have reviewed and asked questions about their graded exams. The surveys are anonymous, and students are strongly encouraged to be honest with themselves and their instructor.

Sometimes students will admit that the exam content and difficulty were as expected, but they simply did not study. Other times, students indicate they found a section of course material especially difficult or were confused by exam instructions. Such information can be used to improve exam construction and focus class time on difficult topics. Survey responses can also be used to facilitate class discussions on study strategies and exam-taking. Allowing students to write about their frustration with a poor grade has a calming effect. When calmer, students are better able to think clearly and critically about their own study habits and level of preparation for the exam.

Allowing students to write about their frustration with a poor grade has a calming effect.

60

Possible survey questions:

1. What was your exam score? Is it better, worse, or about the same as usual?
2. Does your score please you, upset you, or is there no reaction (for example, "I don't care")?
3. Was your test score what you expected? Why or why not?
4. Write the number missed for each of the following types of items: multiple choice, matching, essay. Did you perform better on some types of questions than on others?
5. Was the content of the test what you expected? Explain.
6. Was the difficulty of the test about what you expected, or was it harder or easier than you expected?
7. On which, if any, of the following types of questions did you do best? Questions based:
    a. only on class material
    b. only on text materials
    c. on both class and text materials
8. How much time did you spend studying for the exam (not including weekly class preparation such as reading or doing homework)?
9. How did you study for the exam (for example, rereading text and notes, making cards, talking about material in study groups or with your instructor, waiting to study until the night before)?
10. How many days have you been absent? How did you make up for missed classes?
11. What is your goal for the next exam?
12. How do you plan to achieve your goal?
13. What can your instructor do to help you achieve your goal?

**Angela Becker, Psychology, IU Kokomo,
and Donna McLean, Speech Communications, IU Kokomo**

'Just' an opinion paper?

One day early in the semester, after explaining the first paper assignment to a humanities class for premed students, I asked for questions. From the back row came a slightly exasperated query: "So, is this just an opinion paper?"

It stopped me for a second and raised my defenses. Was the answer yes or no? I quickly decided that it was both. "Yes," I said; I was asking for their opinion, some synthesis they couldn't find in books, but no, it wasn't just opinion. In humanities classes, opinion is more important, more valid, than my student's question implied.

What's at stake here is the proper relation between facts and interpretation. Every academic field has its guidelines for this relation, and good students learn them. Things get complicated, however, when students who are trained in one field (in this case, the sciences) are required to perform in another (the humanities). In science training, individual opinion is suppressed in favor of the results of objective observation. In undergraduate humanities courses where the materials to be studied and the questions we ask about them are not easily reducible to the factual level, opinion is the appropriate mode of investigation and reporting, and we could not do without it.

61

In the humanities, judgments about quality of opinion take the place of the fact versus opinion distinctions in the sciences. What I look for in papers are not facts or completely objective results, but coherent, relevant, balanced, and well-supported opinions. These qualities together make up our version of objectivity. My student's question was a good one because it led me to clarify this important disciplinary difference for the class.

John Woodcock, English, IU Bloomington

'The totalitarian classroom'

I have found that students often are unaware of the "rules" that govern their own classroom behavior and performance. One way of making one set of rules transparent is to engage your students in a social role-playing game called "The Totalitarian Classroom." It's particularly effective when used on the first day of class.

The teacher announces to students that the course will start off with "The Good Student Game." The teacher should point out that it's a game most if not all of the students are aware of, so they should have no trouble playing it and winning. Indeed, the winner will be "the best student". The teacher should make sure that the chairs or desks are arranged in theater style—no circles or groups, please. Three students are asked to volunteer for special roles; playing the game already, most students will willingly agree to take them on. These special roles are: 1) "Mr./Ms. Yes," who must agree with any statement when asked to comment; 2) "Mr./Ms. No," who must disagree with any statement when asked for a response; and 3) the "Scribe," who must not only take notes of the class discussion, but must be ready to read them back to the class on the teacher's demand. The game begins in earnest when the teacher announces that the class will start by discussing the question: "What is a good student?"

Only students who raise their hands are recognized by the teacher, soon squelching any spontaneous ad libs, and the tension in the room increases when the teacher begins to ask students not to respond with their own ideas, but to compare and comment on the answers of two or more of their peers who have already responded. They must listen— not a bad idea—but will have little time to formulate their own answers. The "Scribe" soon cannot contribute to the arguments but must constantly take notes, or he or she will be embarrassed by the teacher's requests for discussion updates. Frequently, the flow of discussion is diverted by the teacher's asking the "No" and "Yes" students to respond to points made by their colleagues, often forcing them into untenable positions to keep agreeing or disagreeing. Their fellow students generally move in for the "kill" at those times. The

> *Most [students] note how inhumane the authoritarian, controlled discussion has been.*

game (mercifully) ends when one student (usually one playing a designated role, but it can be anyone) throws in the towel and says, in effect, that he or she can't keep up or continue playing. Believe me, this always happens, and quickly, if the teacher keeps a relentless pace.

At that point, the class and the teacher can engage in a lively, open discussion of classroom strategies and teaching and learning styles. Most students recognize they have just experienced and modeled behavior that they don't think represents what a really good student does. Most note how inhumane the authoritarian, controlled discussion has been, although (don't be surprised) some students are quite attuned to and prefer it! Others identify the specific pedagogical strategies that function as barriers to both independent thinking and collaborative learning, and virtually all will remember being in classes just like this one.

What are the outcomes? If you try this game and slip into a more totalitarian style later in the semester (or whenever a student acts like "Mr./Ms. No" or "Mr./Ms. Yes"), you'll find that the rest of the class is sure to remark upon it! Clearly, they have gained a heightened awareness of teaching styles and classroom "rules" and their own roles as student learners.

Eileen T. Bender, English, IU South Bend

Creating a future

In a large freshman course on the History of Images of the Future, I decided to begin with an exercise in which students had to consider their own futures over the next three months. I had given them readings that discussed how to get an overview of a course from the syllabus, books, and the course Web page. The first part of the assignment was to use these techniques to describe what my course would be like over the remainder of the semester. I then asked the students to list three personal goals that they hoped to further by means of the course. Finally, I asked students to look over all of their courses, work schedules, and extracurricular activities for the semester, fill in a schedule for this time period, and describe the points at which they expected to be challenged. While some students, not unsurprisingly, resisted the exercise, others seemed to appreciate the reminder of how important scheduling would be for their success in college and to take some responsibility for their own success or failure.

David Pace, History, IU Bloomington

Argument? Discussion? What's the difference?

There are many valid goals for discussion in college humanities classes, but a few years ago I was shocked to realize that my students had not understood one goal that was particularly important to me.

I was teaching a first-year class with an ethics component, so early on students had been exposed to the idea of individual diversity and the operating principles of tolerance and respect. However, I woke up in the middle of class one day to see that my students, when I asked them to discuss an idea, spent virtually all their time arguing—that is, trying to prove that they were right and others were wrong!

At that point I saw an opportunity to clarify something of importance to that class and, I believe, to all humanities discussion classes: a function for discussion that was separate from argument. Argument certainly has its place as a testing ground for ideas and evidence, but its hard-edged and adversarial qualities seem to work against multiplicity and can drive some kinds of knowledge into hiding.

In reaction against what I had seen, I defined the role of discussion as investigative

63

rather than argumentative, with its goal being not to defeat someone who had a different idea but rather to discover in as much detail as possible how someone else understood that idea and how it fit into their view of the world. A final goal, once an alien-seeming idea had been understood, would be to judge the relation of that idea to one's own ideas and possibly incorporate some or all of it. Defined this way, discussion seems to me more likely than argument to facilitate intellectual, personal, and ethical growth.

John A. Woodcock, English, IU Bloomington

A syllabus for active inquirers

At the undergraduate level, I have taught a pre-service teacher education course on school and society. I also teach an education and social issues course for a special cohort group of students seeking both a master's degree and teacher certification. During the very first week of class, I arrange for students to determine what the course content will be for the last month or so of the semester. The students form groups around the issues they have selected; these groups are responsible for determining readings and teaching the topic to their classmates. I play the role of resource person, helping the students delimit the subject and design the activities that will illuminate the issues in meaningful ways. A debriefing after the session with the presenting students helps them evaluate the extent to which they were successful in achieving their educational goals.

Structuring courses in this way accords both with my own philosophy of teaching and with current pedagogical notions of engaging students so they assume greater responsibility for their education. Such instructional approaches are more likely to contribute to the formation of individuals who are active inquirers and of future teachers who are inclined to structure learning environments that are more active, participatory, collaborative, student-centered, and democratic.

These adjectives reflect basic components of my philosophy of teaching and the way I go about organizing my course content and classroom activities. Being something of an existentialist, I also like the challenge of continually creating meaning as I interact with my students to make sense of the world. Besides, this approach to classroom organization—building on the interests of the students and trusting them to take responsibility for a substantial portion of instructional activities—makes the multiple tasks of teaching easier, more enjoyable, and endlessly variable. It also means that I, too, am cast in the role of learner—and this love of learning is perhaps the main reason I am a teacher.

Robert Arnove, Education, IU Bloomington

Shifting responsibility for learning

My goal in teaching is to get students to buy into the idea that learning is their responsibility. In order to emphasize the importance of this idea, I will, regardless of the class, usually spend the entire first session discussing the process of teaching and learning. We return to the topic periodically throughout the semester.

I start the first session of each of my classes in politics and public policy by asking the students about their best and worst classroom experiences. We then move to trying to figure out what constitutes a productive teaching-learning environment. Invariably, the best classroom experiences have been ones where students have felt involved in the class, have taken some ownership in mastering course content, and have been able to share their perspectives with others.

I declare up front that I judge the relative success or failure of the class not on how well students do on exams or research projects, but rather on how much I learn in the class. I reason that if I carry away new knowledge, most of the students will as well. We learn by relating students' own experiences with government and politics to a body of scholarly knowledge offered within a theoretical framework. I provide the theory and scholarly insight; they provide the experience that collectively is greater than my own.

> *The major emphasis in all of my classes is on shared responsibility for teaching and learning, on collaboration rather than competition.*

In the first session, we go around the room and discuss everyone's background and how each of us can contribute to the teaching-learning process. The message is that, during the course of the semester, it will be the responsibility of all students to see to it that the rest of us benefit from their own individual experiences. To help, we go through the syllabus and briefly discuss each topic that will be covered during the semester. I then try to relate these topics to the personal and professional experiences that the students have discussed.

Although different courses call for different approaches, the major emphasis in all of my classes is on shared responsibility for teaching and learning, on collaboration rather than competition. I want students to talk to each other and to learn from each other.

Students, of course, will invariably also bring their prejudices and incomplete or misinterpreted information to class. The danger is that these views get reinforced by other students rather than dispelled. This danger can be alleviated, however, by the presentation of relevant facts and the open discussion of alternative ideas. The more the students themselves undertake these tasks, the greater the impact is likely to be. It is when prejudicial views begin to change that I know the "real" learning is taking place.

If students buy into the idea that they are responsible for their own learning, they will, in fact, learn, and so will I.

William P. Hojnacki, School of Public and Environmental Affairs, IU South Bend

Exams as diagnostic tools

Before I pass back the first exams, I talk to students about how they can learn from them. We talk about using exams as diagnostic tools, not just as assessments. I pass back the correct answers to each question (I use the best student answers for essays), and I encourage students to look at their exams carefully to see why they had wrong answers. I also give them the following handout:

Learning from the exam

1. Compare the correct answers on the answer sheet to your test paper. Check over the math. Did I make any clerical errors? If so, let me know immediately.

2. Compare the correct answers to your own. Do you think that you should receive

65

more points for a particular answer? If so, WRITE DOWN your reason. Be as specific as possible, referring to page numbers or lecture notes. Return your entire exam and your written reason to me. I will look over your paper this week. Next week, I will return the paper with a note telling whether I changed the grade, and why.

3. Look at your pattern of errors. Did you have more trouble with multiple choice vs. essay? Definitions, applications, theories? A particular chapter? Book versus lecture? Did you have trouble understanding or remembering the material? Did you know the material but have trouble answering the questions? Pinpointing your problems will help you find a solution.

4. Think back to your learning behaviors. How did you take notes, study for the test, make up your "exam card"? Did you highlight the text efficiently? Use the study guide? Study with others? How effective were these behaviors? Were you too anxious to think? Can you think of improvements for the future?

5. Were there any other factors that affected your performance? Family crises, learning disabilities, etc.? Were these one-time events, or are they likely to cause problems in the future? What can you do to alleviate these problems?

6. If your test performance was not what you wanted, TAKE ACTION! Figure out what the problem is, and get help with a solution. You have a number of resources: me, family and friends, classmates, the Counseling Center, etc. I will be happy to talk to you, if there is any way I can help. But the responsibility for actions is YOURS.

Gwynn Mettetal, Education, IU South Bend

Weaning students from dependency

If we want to foster the personal development of our students, if we want to help them become intellectually mature human beings, to become independent learners, equipped and eager to pursue self-directed, lifelong learning, we need to wean them from their dependence on us.

Twelve to 16 years of American public education conditions students to believe the professor is the authority and should tell them what to do, how to do it, and whether they did it well or poorly. Who among us has not cringed at the comment: "Just tell me what you want me to do"?

Fostering such obeisance might produce docile employees for authoritarian bosses, but it does not prepare our students to become independent, creative problem-solvers. One effective tool for weaning students from their dependency on us and helping them become their own authority figures is Student Self-Evaluation.

What Student Self-Evaluation looks like. I require self-analyses for all assignments in my visual communications courses. The following excerpt, from an assignment in my computer publication design course, explains the rationale.

> **Written component.** The fastest way to improve your computer and design skills is to develop the habit of self-criticism. Reflect on what you were trying to accomplish and how well you succeeded, what you did right that should be repeated, and what didn't work that needs adjusting. To help you develop this self-criticism, I want you to write an analysis of your

work. It should be a minimum of one typewritten or computer printout page, but you are encouraged to write more. Besides responding to the above ideas, you might relate your creative process, explain your solutions, point out subtleties I might miss, and enumerate problems you encountered. You might also say how you would improve your work if you had time to do it again. Stated another way, tell me what you want me to know about your process that's not visible in your product.

For this same course, I assign a learning evaluation essay that asks students to reflect on their learning for the entire semester. It reads in part:

Self-reflection. Self-analysis. Self-criticism. Self-evaluation. Whatever you choose to call it, the act of stepping outside yourself and examining your thoughts and your work is a valuable habit to cultivate as you prepare yourself for life-long learning. Soon you will leave higher education where professors and peers give you constructive criticism on how to improve your work, your skills, yourself. If you are lucky, you might find a boss who will take an interest in your personal and professional development, but most supervisors are too busy to be your teacher. Most of what you learn after school you must teach yourself. Most improvement in your work and your life you must generate.

To help you develop the habit of self-evaluation, I ask you to critique each computer design assignment. The rationale for this essay is the same as for those critiques. Only the scope is different. I want you to reflect on your learning for the entire semester. If you have never thought about yourself as a learner, never studied your learning style, this is an opportunity to begin.

> **Public education conditions students to believe the professor is the authority and should tell them what to do, how to do it, and whether they did it well or poorly.**

Student Self-Evaluation performs several valuable functions for students. It helps them focus on their learning process instead of their products. It puts psychological distance between them and their work. It helps them internalize standards. It fosters meta-cognition, that is, thinking about their thinking and monitoring their problem-solving process.

Student self-evaluation is also valuable for teachers. It is a major tool to assess students' learning. It lets us respond to our students' processes, not just to their products. It lets us empathize with their fears, frustrations, and triumphs.

Two cautions in using student self-evaluation: We should separate grades from feedback and use student self-evaluations only for feedback. Second, we should not automatically agree with students who are extremely harsh about their work.

The primary source on this teaching-learning strategy is: MacGregor, Jean, ed., "Student Self-Evaluation: Fostering Reflective Learning," *New Directions for Teaching and Learning* series, No. 56, San Francisco: Jossey-Bass, 1993.

Claude Cookman, Journalism, IU Bloomington

67

Teaching to learn

I believe that the best way to learn and retain a difficult concept is by teaching it. So, a few times during the semester, after covering a new concept or idea, I require each student to find someone to teach that concept to outside the class. Students can choose anyone above a certain age (say age 10), who has never taken the course—a parent, a friend, another teacher, a roommate, or the person behind them in the supermarket line. They are expected to write reports about their teaching experiences. How did they go about it? What examples did they use? How did they test their students' comprehension? The students' benefits from this practice are visible, and they all admit to its effectiveness. My benefit from reading the reports, however, is far greater. The students display ingenious ways of introducing a new notion, humorous and down-to-earth examples for its applications, and excellent assessment techniques. I recommend this exercise enthusiastically.

> *I require each student to find someone to teach that concept to outside the class.*

Leah Savion, Philosophy, IU Bloomington

Helping students reframe criticism

All too often, students read constructive criticism as "failure," and they grow frustrated or angry over their poor performances. For those of us who seek to offer criticism without discouraging or alienating our students, this can be a problem. The question is how to solve it.

One thing that I have found helpful, in addition to providing plenty of positive feedback as to what students are doing right, is to talk explicitly with students about the importance of learning how to treat constructive criticism and even negative feedback as information. People who succeed in their careers, who succeed in life, have learned how to do this. They operate on the assumption that when things go wrong, there probably is something in the experience that they can learn from. They look for that something, and they do not allow failure to derail them.

Often I confide to the students that I am one who has had to learn this life skill the hard way—long after I left the classroom. I let them know, from my own personal experience, how important it will be for them to acquire this skill before they get into the job market. It usually is not difficult, after such self-disclosure, to prompt students to notice how they themselves typically respond to poor grades or criticism. Are they crushed? Do they lose their momentum? Do they get angry and use that anger as fuel? Whatever their responses to criticism (and they don't need to tell me if they don't want to), they can be prompted to reflect on how their reactions work for them. To the extent that they don't work, most students are willing to listen to suggestions for reframing the "failure" into something they can use.

I have received numerous letters from alumni over the years who have been grateful for the lessons they learned about receiving criticism in my classroom. I am always reminded, when I receive such letters, that we not only teach our subjects, we teach life skills as well.

S. Holly Stocking, Journalism, IU Bloomington

Imparting the courage to fail

Franz Kafka said that the artist (and it also applies to anyone engaged in any creative activity) must avoid impatience and laziness. It is mandatory to do as much as can be done as frequently as it can be done. No magic, no short cuts, no theoretical pretentious posturing, no excuses—just do it, dammit. Mark Twain said that familiarity breeds more than contempt, it also breeds children, and I add that it also breeds self-contained deep satisfaction in real skill developed and realized. The student will at times fail, so what? The teacher should impart to the student the courage to fail and to continue. It is by failure that one learns and grows, not by modest success.

Harold Zisla, Arts (Retired), IU South Bend

Practice, practice, practice

According to many of our students, introductory economics is one of the tougher courses they face in their early college years. I tell my students that shouldn't be too surprising. The analytical skills needed to do well in economics are similar to those one would have had to use in high school algebra classes, and those classes weren't that easy either.

Along these lines, it is not unusual for students to come to me quite frustrated with their performance in the class. They note that they attend class regularly, take good notes, understand the lectures and their notes but then can't do as well on the exams as they expect they should.

The last few years, I have discussed this problem on the first day of class. I've tried the following analogy, and the students seem to get the point: I ask if they sing along with the radio as they drive along in their cars. The response is an overwhelming "yes." I then ask them how many could sing the song if their radios were to suddenly go quiet. Most nod, affirming, "I get your point."

This year in class, I added the twist of actually playing a well-known Elvis Presley hit and getting the students to sing along. I then shut off the tape player and asked them to keep singing (which was interesting with a class of 350 students). They couldn't (except for Miranda in the back row, who had a very nice voice). Again, they seemed to get the point.

I then went back to explaining how understanding the tools needed to work economics problems is like being able to work those "word" algebra problems. It takes practice, practice, practice—without the music playing.

James Walker, Economics, IU Bloomington

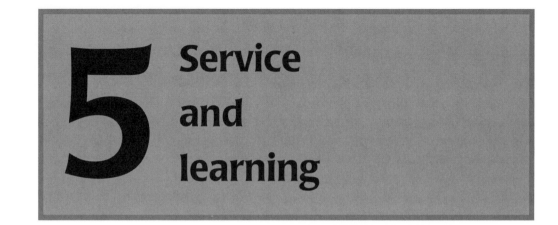

5 Service and learning

It's not enough to sit safely in our ivory towers any more. Our constituencies, including our students, want us to become involved more in the direct workings of our communities. We, too, may want to become more involved in making the world a better place. How can we involve ourselves while preserving and enhancing the learning process? We plan. We work with community agencies to discover their needs. We put our own needs on the table. We negotiate. Together we create activities that are of benefit both to the community and to our students. As teachers, we help our students to reflect on these experiences and the understandings we want them to learn. Students' and community workers' observations, in turn, enrich our own academic understandings. In this way, service-learning is not just for communities, and it's not just for students; it is for all of us.

Pro bono public relations promotes learning

Service-learning provides a great way to accomplish a variety of important aims simultaneously. Students apply the principles and theories covered in the classroom to real problems and needs in the community and gain personal knowledge in the process. They take their learning more seriously and work harder when they know that their work will actually be used. Students also gain a greater appreciation for theory and principles because they can see their utility first hand. I'm also convinced that students retain their learning longer because the service-learning experience is so much more involving than a typical classroom activity. Finally, students typically feel a great sense of accomplishment, knowing that their work has actually benefitted the community. The community and the instructor also gain. Charitable organizations receive help they could not otherwise afford, and the instructor has the satisfaction of teaching students and helping the community at the same time.

The major assignment in my Public Relations Campaigns course is to design and implement a public relations campaign for a local charitable organization. The first step is to identify and contact several charitable organizations that have a need for what my students learn in class. The semester prior to the class, I meet with representatives of the potential client organizations to negotiate the activities and timelines students will follow during their learning experiences. Specific responsibilities and expectations are clearly defined for myself, my students, and the charitable organizations.

When class begins, students are assigned to one of several team projects. I've found that teams of three to five students work best. One student in each team is designated as the leader. The leader's duties include maintaining regular contact with me and with the client organization. In addition to weekly in-class discussion of progress on the campaigns, the class also maintains regular contact via an e-mail discussion list. At the conclusion of the term, each team produces a final written report and presents an oral report to the class and to representatives of their client organization.

> *Students typically feel a great sense of accomplishment knowing that their work has actually benefitted the community.*

Finally, students are asked to write an individual paper on the role of community service from an individual, university, and employer perspective. I ask them to reflect on the importance of building a strong community and to think about ways that they can continue their service and urge current and future employers to serve their communities.

Jeff Springston, Journalism, IUPUI

The community as a learning resource

The local community provides a tremendous learning resource and a wonderful way to connect academic analysis and real-world problems. This is a potential I am just beginning to tap, and I have found it can apply to a wide range of topics.

In Sociology of the Family, my students do short-term service projects at agencies and programs such as Head Start, child advocacy and parental support agencies, women's shelters, and so forth, and then write responses reflecting on the changing needs of families and the demands of family diversity. The volunteer coordinators come to class as guest speakers, and we make one site visit before students select their project location. In Social Stratification, the class meets out in the community three times—at a homeless center, a Latino community center, and a community development corporation. In Race and Ethnic Relations, visits to community groups are coupled with a range of optional activities at ethnic churches, community centers, and neighborhood groups.

I have begun to draw on community resources for less obvious topics as well. In Culture and Society, some students use a nearby campus art museum to reflect on the interrelationship of art, religion, and daily life, and visit the United Nations Store and a self-help crafts outlet to look at indigenous handicrafts and the global economy. They also write short ethnographies of local "microcultures." In International Inequality and Development, students have talked with area employers and labor leaders coping with the overseas transfer of industrial production. There are no doubt many other ways students can learn to think globally as they investigate locally.

Scott Sernau, Sociology, IU South Bend

Fostering reflection about service

Students engaged in service-learning projects need to regularly practice the skill of reflecting about how the hands-on experiences they are getting relate to the skills and content we want them to garner from the course.

A technique that I have found quite useful in this regard is called "Exit Cards." Although the name is rather generic, the purpose is not. Students are asked to purchase a pack of notecards at the beginning of the semester. At the end of every class period, they are required to turn in an exit card. On the cards, I require students to make at least one connection between the content covered that day and their service experience.

At first, the students find this difficult. Many of them have to spend several moments after class trying to come up with a connection. I write personal and detailed responses on each of these cards, noting good connections and suggesting other connections that come to mind as I think about their projects and the content.

As students progress through the course and their service projects, they begin to have a much easier time making these connections. I often notice students grabbing their cards in the middle of class and jotting things down as the proverbial light bulbs go off.

Randall Osborne, Psychology, IU East

Service-learning in a community project

Initiatives such as cooperative learning, collaborative learning, learning communities, project-based learning, and service-learning are often touted as cure-alls for a host of problems ranging from poor student involvement in learning to low rates of student persistence. While a good deal of anecdotal evidence is available to support proponents' claims about effectiveness of such initiatives, in general, empirical evidence is lacking.

The need to assess such programs provided the impetus for a pilot service-learning project involving the rehabilitation of an abandoned 100-year-old house. A group of students enrolled in a senior-level construction engineering design course elected to tackle the redesign project in lieu of the traditional "Semester-End Design Project." Students were involved in all phases of construction and design development; in addition, they were required to make presentations, submit progress reports to community agencies involved, and meet with the neighborhood association to keep residents abreast of the work. Two students from the group registered for a one-credit service-learning option and were required to maintain a diary to reflect upon their service activities.

> **Do service-based learning programs make a difference in student learning? And if so, how?**

There have been several outcomes of this service-based learning project. A paper was jointly presented at an American Society for Engineering Education conference by one of the students and the professor. In addition, once reconstruction of the house was completed, it was sold to a qualified low-income, "first-time" home buyer.

Building upon the success of this pilot service-based course and the enthusiasm of the students, we have now expanded this course. Students in the revised course will be asked to develop floor plans to convert an 80-year-old, two-story structure into a three-bedroom house, following today's codes and standards. The expanded course design also incorporates such concepts as service-based learning, team-building, across-the-curriculum teams (involving interior design, architecture, construction, and civil engineering), and cooperative learning through interaction with team members, community agencies, and a steering committee that will meet with the students to monitor progress, provide assistance, and lend support.

While we have already gained evidence of the positive aspects of service-learning through these course activities, we are now seeking the answers to two crucial questions: Do service-based learning programs make a difference in student learning? And if so, how do these programs make a difference?

Through gathering campuswide data, we intend to compare the experience and performance of students in service-based learning courses and those in nonservice-based learning classes to provide additional answers about the impact of such efforts on student learning.

Sanjiv Gokhale, Construction Technology, IUPUI

Community service-writing

A major challenge for writing instructors is to help students develop the skills they need to become effective and reflective writers. In my course, Writing for a Better Society, I do so by combining community service with writing. Students volunteer at a community agency and write an assignment for public use by the agency. Writing assignments include a brochure that describes agency mission and services, a volunteers' manual, an article for the agency newsletter, fact sheets on timely issues, announcements of coming events, descriptions of new programs, and "bios" of agency staff members. Through their service, students come to know the agency and to find a context for their writing. In

73

turn, the knowledge and skills they gain from their service-writing are applied to their final course assignment, a research paper. In special cases where the writing involves agency-directed research, students have the option of using their service-writing as part of their research paper.

As I see it, there are three distinct advantages to service-writing. First, the prospect of writing for real people on issues affecting their everyday lives is deeply appealing to students. Many students are exploring consciously, for the first time, the attitudes, interests, and needs of their audiences, and ways of reaching them. Second, students often use their academic learning when they perform service related to their disciplines. In writing, students learn to apply theoretical concepts to practical situations and to translate specialized information into accessible knowledge for the community. My role as instructor is to formulate appropriate questions that would lead students, in individual analysis and group discussion, to reflect on their service writing and their role as writers. Finally, service-writing helps students take pride in their writing, as it must meet the standards of professional publication.

> *Writing for real people on issues affecting their everyday lives is deeply appealing to students.*

Because agency requirements vary, some students end up doing more research and writing than others. In dealing with this discrepancy, I emphasize the rhetorical skills that students learn in common, so that they come to value these skills and to understand that real-world projects are seldom as uniform as course assignments.

Joan Pong Linton, English, IU Bloomington

Service-learning: Building an ethic of caring

A women's studies practicum is a fine example of how women's studies and service-learning have intersecting visions of building an ethic of caring. Women's studies courses always attempt to address the "woman's situation" from a critical perspective, and gender provides a special lens on the social issues students encounter in both their placements and their research. The practicum provides a collaborative context for both action and reflection. The ultimate question each practicum student addresses is how hierarchies and institutional power can be confronted so that better services can be rendered to women.

The first class meeting focuses on each student's area of interest and on community organizations where students may possibly pursue a practicum project. We emphasize having students seek their own placements; in a service-learning course, establishing their own placements is just as important for the students as doing their own research and writing their own papers. Of course, the instructor will assist any students who try but do not find the community placement they had targeted. Practicum students are required to keep a reflective journal about their placement activities.

The second class meeting occurs after each student has performed 10 hours of service and focuses on the volunteer experiences and the sharing of students' journals. We discuss the type of service the community organization is attempting to provide and how

74

successfully the organization seems to be meeting the needs of the women it serves. Students are then encouraged to begin their research. They are instructed not to be critical during their on-site volunteer work but to assess that work in their research and to suggest ways to improve the delivery of services.

The third class meeting occurs after students have completed their 40 hours of service (a letter from the organization confirming the hours served is required). The course then focuses on how students have integrated their experiences with their research. At the final class meeting, students present their research papers. These papers are always mutually enlightening. Practicum students have volunteered at Planned Parenthood, the YWCA, Catholic Charities, women's health and counseling centers, battered women's shelters, homeless centers, juvenile detention centers, and literacy programs, and they have shared their knowledge with the community and with one another. While providing needed services to a particular agency, these students have also established a critical framework for community leadership and social action.

Patricia McNeal, Women's Studies, IU South Bend

Environmental action and service projects

I present my class with the opportunity to improve the environment in which they live, through either an environmental action project or a service-based project. Students may work individually or collaboratively on a group project. Drawing upon the different backgrounds and talents of the students, the opportunities for a wide variety of projects are virtually unlimited. I provide a list of previous projects and ideas based on areas of interest.

The action projects have ranged from planting wildflowers at an arboretum to a river cleanup. The areas of interest have included art (designing a series of environmental posters and T-shirts), business (helping local businesses with environmental projects), engineering (developing a model that demonstrated an environmental principle), law (working with law enforcement officials in improving compliance with environmental laws), media (reporting and videotaping an environmental problem or controversy and interviewing representatives of the organizations involved), medical (presenting information on toxins, local health effects of pollution, or natural alternative therapies to community groups), music/dance (composing a musical score about an environmental issue and performing it before a community group), and urban planning (initiating a project involved in "greening" the community through tree plantings and community gardens). I emphasize to the students that the projects should teach themselves, fellow students, and me something about environmental problem-solving while being an issue of personal importance to the students. They should be fun for the students as well.

> *The action projects have ranged from planting wildflowers at an arboretum to a river cleanup.*

I strongly encourage students to do a service project where they volunteer their services to an organization. Important criteria for service projects in my courses include selecting a project that deals with a meaningful environmental issue, collaborating with a

75

contact person/supervisor at the organization in planning the project and working with that person in carrying out the project, and making sure the project is satisfactorily completed by discussing it with the organization's contact person. I stress to my students that it is important to remember that they are working in cooperation with another organization that will depend on the students to do a good job. This means that all students involved should be committed to doing the best job possible since their performance will not only affect their grades, but also have an impact on the opportunities of students in the future.

> *Many students recognize that what they learn can be used to accomplish something of practical value.*

At the end of the course, each group hands in one group-written scientific paper. The group also presents its project to the class. I encourage them to think about using audiovisual aids such as slides, videotapes, and transparencies in their presentations to better keep everyone mentally engaged. One of the central themes of the course is that students have not done science until they have presented their data and interpretations in a way that is usable by colleagues.

Not surprisingly, students develop their greatest depth of knowledge in areas central to their projects. The two most successful aspects of these projects, however, have been that many students recognize that what they learn can be used to accomplish something of practical value and that they begin to understand the mechanics of collaborative efforts. I believe many students initially look at service-learning projects as "classwork" and simply prefer this type over more traditionally structured ones. Somewhere during the service-learning project, however, many come to realize that what they have learned is valuable and that they can have a role in solving local environmental problems. Personally, the most rewarding aspect of these projects is the shift in student focus from the importance of the project's grade to the importance of their participation in solving community problems.

Neil Sabine, Biology, IU East

LeaderLab

One of my courses, Managing and Behavior in Organizations, includes a service-learning initiative that I call LeaderLab. At the start of the course each term, some very high-performing students are competitively selected for leadership opportunities in nonprofit organizations. The goal is twofold: 1) to provide a select number of students with an opportunity for leadership in a "real-world" context in a way that provides a laboratory for application of management skills learned in class, and 2) to infuse local service organizations (for example, United Way and Hoosiers for Higher Education) with some motivated student leaders. I try to make the experience a "laboratory" by asking each of the participants to publicly establish, in a presentation to the entire class, a charter for what they hope to accomplish in their projects. These students must also provide the class with interim reports and a final summary of their experiences.

I have found that, unlike other non-compensated opportunities with which I have experimented, the public nature of LeaderLab creates real accountability for getting something accomplished and therefore makes it more likely that the students will actually contribute something. Indeed, I think the program has been a win-win-win situation—that is, a positive experience for the LeaderLab students, the other students in my course, and the participating organizations.

First, I think that this program has been a growth experience for the selected LeaderLab students. Over the years, I have found that the topics we cover in my course—teams, motivation, leadership—are relatively easy to understand but very difficult to apply effectively. The LeaderLab experience places students in a position where they have to apply some of the skills they've learned in class to accomplish their projects, and the complexity of doing so turns out to be a challenging and powerful learning experience, hard to duplicate in a classroom setting.

Second, the other students in my course are very much interested in learning about the LeaderLab students' experiences. There is just something about hearing from people of their own age and background that they find intriguing and relevant. I think it is much easier for them to project themselves into the roles of the LeaderLab students than some of the other organizational examples we use in class.

Finally, I think the program has been a plus for the service organizations for which the students have worked. While our liaison administrators at the organizations are always tight on time, the chance to meet and work with talented young people is something they all embrace. In short, I think the manifestation of service-learning we employ in my course has been a success, and I enthusiastically endorse the concept of service-learning.

Timothy Baldwin, Business, IU Bloomington

Passing the torch

A course that involves a service-learning component often sends students to the same site (agency, family, etc.) semester after semester. I have found it useful to have students formally "pass the torch" when this occurs. Students from the previous semester meet for a discussion of the site with the new students for that placement; then the two students visit the site together. This obviously is helpful to the new students who usually gain advance insights about the service-learning site, but it is also helpful to the previous students who then feel more at ease about leaving "their spot" in good hands. It also helps people at the service-learning site feel that a smooth transition is occurring.

> *I have found it useful to have students formally 'pass the torch'.*

Obviously, students have to be told from the start that they are required to make this visit during the next semester. I have never had a student who was unwilling to take the extra time; most are eager for the opportunity for one last visit.

Gwynn Mettetal, Education, IU South Bend

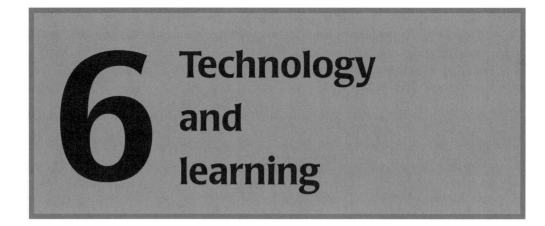

6 Technology and learning

Our students may be a part of the MTV generation, but they don't need to be zombies. With appropriate coaching, they can become more than plugged-in consumers of television and other technologies, both inside and outside the classroom. How can we support them to do this? We can understand that all technologies work best as enhancements of traditionally sound pedagogy, not replacements for it. We also can be active ourselves—in previewing materials, in understanding the technology well enough for its use to become a seamless part of our practice, in raising questions for students to consider, in pausing a film or videotape to take time for much needed reflection, and perhaps most importantly, in fostering relationships and creating community where none seems possible.

Learning from a television miniseries

Some of the most successful classes I have taught were based on a popular television miniseries. My first experiment of this sort was in conjunction with the series "The Winds of War." Together with another professor, I developed an approach that combined television-watching and a conventional history course on World War II.

Since there was a great surge of publicity about this series, we had a huge response from students. It was one of the largest upper-division classes we ever offered, two or three times the size of our usual classes. We were somewhat surprised to find that our students were among the most motivated and successful we had taught. They were required to watch the entire (rather long) miniseries on television, but they also had to read the original book on which it was based. Fortunately, it is an excellent historical novel, one that several department members had previously used in their classes as supplementary reading. Though the series was markedly inferior to the book in many ways, it provided a useful basis for interesting and rewarding classroom discussion. Students could visualize many scenes far better than they could have done from reading the book alone, which was particularly important for those students (and there were many) who learn better by seeing than by reading.

Nothing that I include in my regular World War II class was omitted. The reading assignments were as long and as professional, including two major textbooks and three supplementary paperbacks. The students had to do a research paper and participate actively in class discussions. The results were phenomenal. The discussions were active and well-informed. Virtually all of the students participated in them. The final examinations they wrote were as good or better than those I have seen in any class during my 30 years of teaching at the university level. In a typical upper-level class, I usually give 10 to 15 percent A's. In this class, over half of the students earned A's.

Subsequently, I have taught a number of other courses by this method and find that they work very well. Many excellent miniseries are available on video and can be used periodically, but the excitement and publicity that comes from teaching a class while the series is first being presented on television proved to be very valuable.

Paul H. Scherer, History, IU South Bend

Putting it on the Web

Faculty typically generate a variety of handouts to support their courses. When students miss classes, handouts, and information, it is often difficult and expensive to coordinate replacements.

Posting syllabi and other materials on the World Wide Web makes them accessible on the students' time. Even last semester's syllabus can be a useful tool for students and faculty doing schedule planning.

As an instructor, I have found that looking at what others have done can help me to plan a new course and to equate courses taught at different campuses.

Susan Shapiro, Psychology, IU East

Choosing and using video for learning

I have been impressed with the power of video to make unfamiliar situations, problems, lifestyles, and cultures come to life for my students. I have also been dismayed by the tendency of the television screen to produce passivity in students. They can easily perceive the video as a "movie" to break up the time, rather than as an important learning aid. I have found several techniques to help overcome this:

1. Emphasis on quality. Some truly excellent, insightful, and award-winning films are available. A great deal of mediocre material is also being highly touted for classroom use. I have found it important to preview everything, to select only that which is both very well done and highly appropriate to the class content.

2. Close integration with the rest of the class. The video is preceded by a brief preparatory lecture highlighting things to watch for, or presenting trends, which are then illustrated in the video. The video is followed by class reactions and discussion.

> *Students can easily perceive the video as a 'movie' to break up the time, rather than as an important learning aid.*

3. Short duration. Video clips of 5 to 15 minutes can be very effective in providing a glimpse of another social world. Longer videos can be excerpted or can be stopped for clarification or discussion. A remote control can be useful for this.

4. Explanatory material. An overhead, preferably off to one side or corner, can provide concepts to note, spellings of unfamiliar places and terms, things to watch for, and questions to consider. An out-of-the-way overhead can also be useful for summary or background information for the introductory lecture or follow-up discussion.

5. An assigned response. The video can be followed by an individual response, either an open-ended written question or comment or an answer to a question about content or implications. Group responses, in which a small group discusses one or more questions, have also been very effective. The first-time students often are struck by how much "slipped past" them as they watched. Later, they learn to become more involved, thoughtful viewers (not a bad habit to learn for life as well as class).

Scott Sernau, Sociology, IU South Bend

Better learning through technology?

I have been privileged to use technology in my teaching since 1990, and I remain committed to its power and its possibilities. These are the premises I operate under as I use a given technology or consider an emerging one:

1. The university's role is to move information, not people.
2. Learning should not be bound by place, time, speed of learning, or even learning styles.
3. Learning takes place best when students are actively engaged.
4. The message must mold the medium.

When I find a teaching tool that falls in line with at least some of these, I pay atten-

tion. I find that technology has a wonderful way of potentially addressing all of the above. Of ultimate concern must always be the question: "Does technology help improve student learning?"

A review of the literature indicates that "replacement technologies" (television, video-tapes, CD-ROMs), which simply substitute for a lecture, have a neutral effect on student learning. On the other hand, "engagement technologies" (interactive computer programs, simulations, interactive video discs), which constantly call upon the student's involvement, have a positive effect on student learning. The literature is clear on this point. Other data suggest that:

1. Reading comprehension of difficult material is increased using computer programs.
2. Local area network (LAN)-induced collaborative learning leads to faster learning.
3. Computer modeling improves exam performance.
4. Interactive computer-aided instruction (CAI) improves learning outcomes and speed by 20 percent.
5. Poor students perform considerably better with introduction of hypertext tutoring.
6. Chemistry laboratory scores move from an average 59 to 80 percent with the introduction of an interactive video disc (IVD). Quiz results change from about four out of seven to five out of seven.
7. Computer-based instruction even promotes a more positive attitude.

The amazing fact is that these documented learning gains lie not at all with the technology being used, but rather with long-established, good pedagogies these technologies promote. In fact, it has been shown that any resulting benefits are directly attributable to the teaching method the technology supports.

Just as the printed book half a millennium ago needed about a century to have any significant impact on teaching and learning, so technology will need some time to establish itself. I firmly believe that academe will be well-served if we continue to explore both the strengths and limitations of technology.

Erwin Boschmann, Chemistry, IUPUI

Closing the distance in distance-learning

Having taught a televised Interpersonal Communication course several times that was either broadcast over a local television channel or received by students on videotape, I have developed some techniques that increase student interaction and foster community. These strategies increase chances for student-centered learning in televised courses delivered through distance-education television technology:

1. Personally call and welcome each student enrolled in the course, indicate when they can expect to receive any broadcast, videotapes, or written materials, and offer friendly reminders of the self-discipline needed for televised distance-learning.

2. Hold three to five face-to-face or two-way interactive video class meetings. Saturday morning is a time most people who need distance-education courses are available. An orientation meeting, a meeting before midterm and final, and actual meetings for the two examination dates worked well for me because the time afterward could be used for interactive exercises. Cookies and beverages helped during these face-to-face sessions.

3. Take group photographs of students present at face-to-face meetings and photographs of the monitor for students at distance hookup sites. The names of students can be printed beneath the photographs and sent to all to foster familiarity.

4. Strongly suggest that students in close proximity form study-group sessions among themselves to increase human interaction. Assist by reserving space and equipment on campus, if needed.

5. Require students to complete and hand in or mail in Practices (such as "provide a written analysis to the brief interpersonal case study dialogue exhibited on the screen in Lesson Two"). This encourages application and discourages viewing delays.

6. Aid student pacing of classwork by sending occasional traditional and electronic mailings of assignment reminders and test reviews to students.

7. If facilities allow, travel to the most distant site for instruction at least once so that students farthest away will feel more engaged in the learning process.

8. Maintain definite office hours to receive students' assignments and respond to questions via telephone, facsimile, and e-mail.

9. Store multiple videotape copies of each broadcast lecture in campus and local area libraries for easy student and community access and interaction.

Dorothy W. K. Ige, Communications, IU Northwest

Raiding virtual libraries

For years I have been frustrated because many of the primary sources that I would like to use in history courses include vocabulary and references that are unknown to many of my students. Even when students are actually in a position to understand the text, the unknown elements sometimes convince them that it is beyond them.

I recently discovered the virtual libraries that exist on the Internet. Many of these are accessible through our university's library homepage. The extent of these collections of original materials is already quite impressive and is growing rapidly. As an experiment I downloaded a 19th-century translation of *The Communist Manifesto* and used my word processing program to add in italicized definitions of terms that my students might not know, explanations of references that might be unclear, and general background material establishing the context of the document. I then made this annotated source available to my students on the course Web site, although I might equally well have printed it out for reserve or a course reader.

Through this process, I believe that I may have succeeded in leveling the playing field between those students who come into the class with a good deal of background knowledge and those who do not, and I am now in a position to assign more demanding texts than I felt was appropriate in the past.

David Pace, History, IU Bloomington

Learning on the listserv

I set up a listserv for students in my psychology course to continue discussions outside of class. Messages sent to the list were to consist of reactions to or thoughts about lectures, films, or in-class discussion. I monitored the list occasionally, sent my own questions, replies, and comments, or forwarded messages from other lists to which I subscribe.

Over the course of the semester each student was expected to send 10 messages to the discussion list. They earned one point for each message sent to the list; however, they couldn't get credit for more than four messages during any grading period (the time period between exams) in order to ensure that messages would be spread across the semester. They could send more messages; however, they could only earn four points per grading period, and 10 points total (about 3 percent of their grade) for this activity. They received detailed instructions about how to use e-mail and the listserv, both in class and through handouts.

I loved doing this. The students sent many hundreds of messages all semester long, and I felt that it was a very valuable addition to the class. But I would make the following changes:

1. I would provide a handout on computer etiquette—information about not flaming or using all caps. I would also inform them to be very careful not to be insulting or hurtful toward other students. I think that e-mail may remove some social restrictions on disagreement, and I think students should be urged to be cautious about that.

2. I would give clearer guidelines about not posting personal messages to the list, but sending those separately to the individual involved and keeping the list for class discussion only.

Elaine Blakemore, Psychology, IP Fort Wayne

Classes for the MTV generation

The effective use of technology, I have found, is a key ingredient for a successful class with today's students. My own History of Rock Music classes would certainly not be possible without a good audio and video playback system, and I have found that nearly any available technology—including laserdiscs, computers, and CD-ROMs—can be put to effective use. Computer-literate MTV-era students respond favorably to a level of stimulation that might have seemed overwhelming and disorienting a generation ago. For the technology to be effective, however, it must be as transparent as possible, which necessitates another level of planning for each class and a knowledge of the equipment that is thorough enough to make its use second nature and seamless. A calm backup plan for the inevitable breakdowns is essential as well. On the other hand, one shouldn't feel obliged to use technology with which one is not comfortable. In that case, the technology can prove overwhelming and can easily draw attention to itself and away from the material it is relaying. Nothing is more distracting than watching a teacher fumble with equipment, as I learned from my own painful experience of trying to juggle too many media and seeing my class turn into "Teaching with Technology" rather than a music course.

> *A calm backup plan for the inevitable breakdowns is essential.*

Glenn Gass, Music, IU Bloomington

Creating interactive lectures on video

If you are the creator or author of a televised course, there are ways to create interaction opportunities *within the course content* of the broadcast or videotaped lecture presentation.

83

1. Divide each broadcast in half—Part I and Part II—as a psychological break for students who grew up with television commercial breaks.

2. Prerecord each class session to avoid unpredictable problems associated with live broadcasts (absent students, ill instructor or studio crew, malfunctioning equipment, weather-related cancellations, etc.).

3. Include two mini-sets, side by side, for interest. One may be a podium at which you stand to begin and end lessons. The second set may have a table with chairs for "lecturettes" and discussions with a few students or a guest speaker present on the set.

4. Include two to three senior student majors or a guest speaker on the set for discussion and role-playing interaction (more than that number makes for difficult wide camera shots). First- and second-year students enrolled in the televised course tend to relate well to these peer upper-class television personalities, both on and off camera. (The upper-class students may have an independent study arrangement.)

5. Present interesting verbal and nonverbal content and delivery, including clear, visible text and interesting graphics. Copyrighted and copyright-free picture and videotape sources may include CD-ROMs and the work of students and local artists, guest co-lecturers, and your own creativity. Television production staff can usually help identify sources and provide invaluable technical assistance that should enhance viewer interaction.

6. Ask students to provide oral or written responses to questions or case study scenarios while you pause during the broadcast lecture. Then give the correct answer on the screen.

7. Any graphics or text can be compiled in a hard-copy handbook to aid students' notetaking and future study. This handbook can be a supplement to the regular class text. Refer to specific page numbers in handouts and not during the broadcast taping as the texts may change before you update the television broadcast tapes.

8. Include theme music. Most students quickly become familiar with the music and find it engaging.

Students' written course evaluations and grades earned in my televised course reflect that they learn at approximately the same level as their counterparts in the traditional course format.

Dorothy W. K. Ige, Communications, IU Northwest

Active learning in computer classrooms

Computers can be valuable tools for engaging our students in active learning. Their seductive power can keep students on task for long hours. Well-designed computer assignments can prompt our students to work at such higher cognitive levels as applying skills to new situations, analyzing complex tasks, and synthesizing skills with knowledge to solve problems. Like all technology, computers require abandoning our old, comfortable ways. They force us to rethink our attitudes about learning and adjust our teaching practices. They challenge us to harness their potential to our course objectives.

In six years of teaching computer design courses, I have come to expect a wide range of abilities and comfort levels from students. While their numbers decrease each year, many students still suffer from technophobia. "Computers don't like me," remains a

common lament. At the other extreme are the hardwired elite, who often view our fumbling computer skills with scorn. Keeping average students on pace while challenging the gigawizards and supporting the technophobes is akin to juggling and walking a tight rope at the same time.

Here's a process for teaching complex computer skills:

1. Show a model that uses the new skill. In my courses, such models range from newspaper front pages to type designs to informational graphics.

2. Demonstrate the skill on a computer that projects your monitor to a screen.

3. Talk students through the skill, step by step.

4. Ask students who succeeded with the skill to explore it further while you provide one-to-one coaching for those who did not get it to work.

5. Give students an in-class exercise that lets them apply the skill to achieve different results.

6. Give them a tutorial that integrates the new skill with previously learned skills.

7. Give students an open-ended assignment that lets them synthesize their skills with knowledge and apply both domains creatively to solve problems. In my courses, for example, students combine skills in several software applications with theory about typography, color, and principles of design to create publications for specific audiences. Open-ended assignments allow the technologically adept to set their own learning goals and advance their skills rather than settle for lowest-common-denominator standards.

Here are additional, practical suggestions:

1. Get a coach to help you. The coach assists students with problems while you keep the rest of the class on pace. It is extremely stressful to try to teach and coach at the same time. In addition, if you stop teaching to coach, the better students will quickly be reading e-mail or cruising the Web. It requires a struggle to get the class back on task. If your dean or chair cannot assign a coach, deputize one or more of your advanced students.

2. Build success for technologically challenged students into the very first experiences. Through coaching and other support, ensure that they master the skills from the first day. Gradually withdraw support as they gain skill and confidence.

3. Incorporate asynchronous learning—students working at their own pace—into your course design. This lets you spend most of your time coaching. In the schema above, the last three steps are asynchronous.

> *Keeping average students on pace while challenging the gigawizards and supporting the technophobes is akin to juggling and walking a tight rope at the same time.*

4. Have frequent sharing times where students teach their classmates the skills and heuristics they have discovered.

5. Don't teach software *per se* and don't teach disconnected skills. For faster and deeper learning, teach skills as tools to solve real-world problems in your discipline.

6. During step-by-step instructions, teach from the back of the classroom so you can watch the students' terminals. This lets you adjust your pace to the students' progress.

85

This runs counter to our expectations for eye contact, but students cannot engage in eye contact while they are concentrating on computer screens.

7. Do not try to lecture or use other traditional teaching methods in a computer classroom. You are likely to become frustrated as students surreptitiously work on the machines. For non-computer activities, schedule a traditional classroom. If this is not possible, have students leave their terminals and gather in an open area of the room, or insist that they shut down their machines.

Computers offer great potential for active learning in which students control the pace and sequence of learning, and to some degree even their own objectives. To maximize learning in computer courses, however, we cannot approach them as we do traditional ones. Instead of just presenting knowledge, we must become designers of experiences in which we embed our learning objectives.

Claude Cookman, Journalism, IU Bloomington

Team-teaching at a distance

Recently we taught a dual-site interactive video course, "The Biology of Mental Illness," on two separate campuses, in two classrooms, with an instructor at each site. Since neither of us had ever used this medium before, team-teaching not only enabled us to draw on the expertise of two disciplines, but allowed us to collaborate on identifying and addressing the particular challenges distance-learning presents.

One of those challenges is interactive communication. Certainly we instructors and our students could converse with each other. But part of the subtle nuance of teaching is the ability to read nonverbal signals that often provide the instructor with important clues about the students' understanding of course material. We could focus the camera on student speakers, but unless we zoomed in, it was hard to distinguish, interpret, or respond to their facial expressions.

It also became very apparent at the first class meeting that some students were visual learners but atrocious spellers. Coupled with the fact that the first weeks of the course focused on biological concepts, this left those students in a near-panic. There was a marker board available in both classrooms so students could see the terms as they were being used. But focusing our camera on the board exacerbated the difficulty we were already having of seeing students' non-verbal reactions.

We soon learned that students also need, but usually lack, training in handling the challenges of the distance-learning classroom. Although students normally are quite willing to ask and answer questions in a class, they seemed quite tentative about doing so in this new format. Many of the students would whisper their responses or nod when a yes/no question was asked. In that case, particularly if the camera at the remote site was focused on a document or on the marker board, the "distant" instructor would perceive nothing but silence. The instructor would assume the question had not been heard and would ask it again.

How did we address these challenges? First, to aid each other in receiving nonverbal signals, we worked out a buddy system. When the remote-site instructor was speaking, the local-site instructor would make note of concerned expressions and raised hands. At a natural pause in the presentation, the local-site instructor would raise a "QUESTION" card and follow with comments such as "some students seem puzzled by the last point. Could you perhaps provide another example?" In this way, we each could serve as one another's "eyes and ears."

When it came to addressing the challenge of our visual learners, we found we had to rethink the concept of "chalkboard." Now, when we introduce concepts, we use the document camera to write out information on sheets of paper, encouraging students to take notes right along with the instructor. After the material is presented in this fashion, the instructor at the other site asks students to summarize the information. The document camera is turned off so both sites are in full view, and instructors can focus their camera on students as they present their summaries.

Helping students overcome their reluctance to talk out loud has been more difficult. The fact that the course is also being videotaped further intimidates some students. In addition, some students feel uncomfortable speaking into the microphones. We have tried to alleviate this situation by calling on and mentioning students' names. For example, when a student does offer an answer, the instructor on that site will restate it, using the student's name. Over time, this makes students more comfortable and more likely to speak out, and also helps instructors become more familiar with students' voices. Students smile when we acknowledge their contributions even from afar.

One of the things we have learned in this process is that two heads are better than one when teaching a distance-learning class, particularly the first time. We've also found that students, as well as faculty, need training and experience to perform effectively in a distance-learning classroom.

Joan Lafuze, Biology, IU East, and Randall Osborne, Psychology, IU East

Take me out to the movies

In my social work classes, it's vital for students to gain an understanding of people whose backgrounds are different from their own. Although I use traditional means of teaching about diversity in these classes, I find the most effective way of inviting students to understand human differences is by asking them to watch movies. As a way of inviting students to grasp another person's reality, I ask them to choose a movie about a group that they are not familiar with and to empathize with the character in the movie who is least like themselves.

In written assignments, students discuss such topics as the strengths, values, challenges, stresses, and/or resources in the character, family, and/or the environment. In some classes, students write on the similarities and differences between what they have learned about this group in the professional litera-

> *The most effective way of inviting students to understand human differences is by asking them to watch movies.*

ture, what they learned in childhood, and how the group is portrayed in a certain movie.

Often students have reported that this assignment helped them change their view of a group of people. I remember a particular student whose religious background had taught her to view homosexuality as sinful. Knowing that other social work students might criticize her for this view, she had not discussed her thoughts in class and had not allowed herself to get to know students who identified themselves as homosexual. However, she was willing to watch a movie about a group of lesbians. After watching the movie, she told me that she felt much more comfortable about lesbians and in fact respected and liked the character in the movie. For her, this was an important step in learning to accept differences.

A copy of my movie list follows. It includes movies that focus on diversity from the perspective of oppressed groups. I find these movies useful in helping students broaden their understanding and acceptance of many different groups.

Family challenges

Antonia's Line, Marleen Gorris, 1995
Beau Père, Bertrand Blier, 1982
Breathing Lessons, John Erman, 1993
Boys on the Side, Herbert Ross, 1995
Cries and Whispers, Ingmar Bergman, 1972
The Family Game, Yoshimitsu Morita, 1983
Hannah and Her Sisters, Woody Allen, 1986
Hamlet, Franco Zeffirelli, 1990
The Homecoming, Peter Hall, 1973
I Never Sang for My Father, Gilbert Cates, 1970
In the Name of the Father, Jim Sheridan, 1993
Joy Luck Club, Wayne Wang, 1993
Kramer versus Kramer, Robert Benton, 1979
Mr. Holland's Opus, Stephen Herek, 1995
Nobody's Fool, Robert Benton, 1994
Ordinary People, Robert Redford, 1980
Paradise, Mary Agnes Donoghue, 1991
Postcards from the Edge, Mike Nichols, 1990
A River Runs Through It, Robert Redford, 1992
Sleeping with the Enemy, Joseph Ruben, 1991
Staying Together, Lee Grant, 1989
The Sum of Us, Kevin Dowling and Geoff Burton, 1994
Used People, Beeban Kidron, 1992
What's Eating Gilbert Grape, Lasse Hallstrom, 1994
What's Love Got to Do With It, Brian Gibson, 1993
Who's Afraid of Virginia Woolf, Mike Nichols, 1966

Oppression related to sexual and gender orientation

And the Band Played On, Roger Spottiswoode, 1993
The Birdcage, Mike Nichols, 1995
Boys on the Side, Herbert Ross, 1995
The Crying Game, Neil Jordan, 1987
La Cage Aux Folles, Edouard Molinaro, 1978
Philadelphia, Jonathon Demme, 1993
The Adventures of Priscilla, Queen of the Desert, Stephen Elliott, 1994
The Sum of Us, Kevin Dowling and Geoff Burton, 1994
To Wong Foo, Thanks for Everything, Julie Newmar, Beeban Kidron, 1995
Torch Song Trilogy, Paul Bogart, 1988
The Wedding Banquet, Ang Lee, 1993

Childhood and adolescence

Au Revoir les Enfants, Louis Malle, 1987
Blackboard Jungle, Richard Brooks, 1995
Chariots of Fire, Hugh Hudson, 1981
Cross My Heart, Jacques Fansten, 1991

Diary of Anne Frank, George Stevens, 1959
Dead Poets Society, Peter Weir, 1989
Fanny and Alexander, Ingmar Bergman, 1983
Into the West, Mike Newell, 1992
Lean on Me, John Avildsen, 1989
Little Man Tate, Jodie Foster, 1991
Losing Isaiah, Stephen Gyllenhual, 1995
My Name is Ivan, Andrei Tarkovsky, 1963
Small Change, François Truffaut, 1976

Aging
Antonia's Line, Marleen Gorris, 1995
Driving Miss Daisy, Bruce Beresford, 1989
I Never Sang for My Father, Gilbert Cates, 1970
On Golden Pond, Mark Rydell, 1981
Dance with the White Dog, Glenn Jordan, 1993
Unstrung Heroes, Diane Keaton, 1995

People with alcohol and other drug problems
Arthur, Steve Gordon, 1981
Barfly, Barbet Schroeder, 1987
Clean and Sober, Glenn Gordon Caron, 1988
Come Back Little Sheba, Daniel Mann, 1952
The Country Girl, George Seaton, 1954
Days of Wine and Roses, Blake Edwards, 1962
Drugstore Cowboy, Gus Van Sant, Jr., 1989
Fat City, John Huston, 1972
Harvey, Henry Koster, 1950
Hoosiers, David Anspaugh, 1986
I'll Cry Tomorrow, Daniel Mann, 1955
The Lost Weekend, Billy Wilder, 1945
Losing Isaiah, Stephen Gyllenhaul, 1995
The Morning After, Sidney Lumet, 1986
Only When I Laugh, Glenn Jordan, 1981
A River Runs Through It, Robert Redford, 1992
A Star Is Born, George Cukor, 1954
Tender Mercies, Bruce Beresford, 1983
Under the Volcano, John Huston, 1984
The Verdict, Sidney Lumet, 1982
When a Man Loves a Woman, Luis Mandoki, 1994

Physical, mental, or psychological problems
Article 99, Howard Deutch, 1992
Awakenings, Penny Marshall, 1990
Children of a Lesser God, Randa Haines, 1986
Dream Team, Howard Zieff, 1989
The Doctor, Randa Haines, 1991
The Elephant Man, David Lynch, 1980
Fatal Attraction, Adrian Lyne, 1987
Forrest Gump, Robert Zemeckis, 1994
The Fisher King, Terry Gilliam, 1991
Mr. Holland's Opus, Stephen Herek, 1995
My Left Foot, Jim Sheridan, 1989
One Flew Over the Cuckoo's Nest, Milos Forman, 1975
Paradise, Mary Agnes Donoghue, 1991
Rain Man, Barry Levinson, 1988

Regarding Henry, Mike Nichols, 1991
Sybil, Daniel Petrie, 1976
Three Faces of Eve, Nunnally Johnson, 1957
What's Eating Gilbert Grape, Lasse Hallstrom, 1994
Unstrung Heroes, Diane Keaton, 1995
Zelig, Woody Allen, 1984

African-Americans and Africans in other countries

The Autobiography of Miss Jane Pittman, John Korty, 1974
Boyz 'N the Hood, John Singleton, 1991
The Color Purple, Steven Spielberg, 1985
Chocolat, Claire Dennis, 1989
Cry Freedom, Richard Attenborough, 1987
Cry the Beloved Country, Darrell Roodt, 1995
Do the Right Thing, Spike Lee, 1989
Dry White Season, Euzhan Palcy, 1989
Grand Canyon, Lawrence Kasdan, 1991
Glory, Edward Zwick, 1989
Hoop Dreams, Steve James, 1994
Jungle Fever, Spike Lee, 1991
Lean on Me, John Avildsen, 1989
Lilies of the Field, Ralph Nelson, 1963
Long Walk Home, Richard Pearce, 1990
Losing Isaiah, Stephen Gyllenhaul, 1995
Mississippi Blues, Bertrand Tavernier and Robert Parish, 1987
Mississippi Burning, Alan Parker, 1988
Mississippi Masala, Mira Nair, 1991
The Piano Lesson, Lloyd Richards, 1995
The Power of One, John Avildsen, 1992
A Raisin in the Sun, Bill Duke, 1988
To Kill a Mockingbird, Robert Mulligan, 1962
To Sir with Love, James Clavell, 1967

Women

Antonia's Line, Marleen Gorris, 1995
Agnes of God, Norman Jewison, 1985
Alice Doesn't Live Here Anymore, Martin Scorsese, 1975
Another Woman, Woody Allen, 1988
Autumn Sonata, Ingmar Bergman, 1978
An Unmarried Woman, Paul Mazursky, 1978
Beaches, Garry Marshall, 1988
Boys on the Side, Herbert Ross, 1994
Chantilly Lace, Linda Yellen, 1993
Desperately Seeking Susan, Susan Seidelman, 1985
Educating Rita, Lewis Gilbert, 1983
Enchanted April, Mike Newell, 1992
Entre Nous, Diane Kurys, 1983
Fried Green Tomatoes, Jon Avnet, 1991
Gertrude, Carl Dreyer, 1963
Girlfriends, Claudia Weill, 1978
The Handmaid's Tale, Volker Schlondorff, 1990
Joy Luck Club, Wayne Wang, 1993
Julia, Fred Zimmerman, 1977
A League of Their Own, Penny Marshall, 1992
Like Water for Chocolate, Lumi Cavayos, 1993
Little Women, Gillian Armstrong, 1979

Marie, Roger Donaldson, 1986
Mr. and Mrs. Bridge, James Ivory, 1990
My Brilliant Career, Gillian Armstrong, 1979
Norma Rae, Martin Ritt, 1979
Peggy Sue Got Married, Francis Ford Coppola, 1986
The Piano, Jane Campion, 1992
Places in the Heart, Robert Benton, 1984
Purple Rose of Cairo, Woody Allen, 1985
Roe vs. Wade, Gregory Oblit, 1989
Shirley Valentine, Lewis Gilbert, 1989
Silkwood, Mike Nichols, 1984
Sleeping with the Enemy, Joseph Rubin, 1991
Steel Magnolias, Herbert Ross, 1989
La Strada, Federico Fellini, 1954
Terms of Endearment, James Brooks, 1983
The Turning Point, Herbert Ross, 1977
Thelma and Louise, Ridley Scott, 1991
Two Women, Vittorio De Sica, 1960
Violets are Blue, Jack Fisk, 1986
Virgin Spring, Ingmar Bergman, 1960
What's Love Got to Do with It, Brian Gibson, 1993
A Woman's Tale, Paul Cox, 1992
Working Girls, Lizie Borden, 1987
When a Man Loves a Woman, Luis Mandoki, 1994

Prison life
Shawshank Redemption, Frank Darabont, 1994

Other oppressed groups
American Me, James Olmos, 1992
Black Orpheus, Marcel Camus, 1959
City of Joy, Roland Jaffe, 1992
Dances with Wolves, Kevin Costner, 1990
El Norte, Gregory Nava, 1982
The Emerald Forest, John Boorman, 1984
The Green Wall, Armando Robles Godoy, 1970
Hester Street, Joan Micklin Silver, 1975
Home and the World, Satyajit Ray, 1984
Joy Luck Club, Wayne Wang, 1993
La Bamba, Lou Diamond Phillips, 1987
Living on Tokyo Time, Steve Odazaki, 1987
Los Olividadis, Luis Budduwi, 1950
Map of the Human Heart, Vincent Ward, 1993
The Milagro Beanfield War, Robert Redford, 1988
The Mission, Roland Jaffe, 1986
Pixote, Hector Baneco, 1981
Rashomon, Akira Kurosaua, 1951
Running Brave, Donald Shebib, 1983
Stand and Deliver, Ramon Menendez, 1988
El Super, Leon Ichaso, 1979
West Side Story, Jerome Robbins, 1961
Where the Green Ants Dream, Werner Herzog, 1984

Valerie Nash Chang, Social Work, IUPUI

7 Using assessment and evaluation for learning

For many of our students tests are dreaded things. They are the rods by which they either measure up or fall short. They do not seem to be for learning, and often, especially if a student performs poorly, they create resistance. How can we prevent or minimize the problems? We can show students constructive ways to evaluate their own work. We can involve students in developing their own exams. We can offer no-penalty quizzes and use alternative ways to evaluate work, including mini-journals and one-minute papers. In these and other ways, old and new, we can work to create assessments that don't simply test for learning, but also work to create it.

Evolving peer-review

I have used peer-review as a component of student evaluation in graduate courses for several years. Typically, the students are provided criteria in conjunction with a point system to use in the peer-review of classmates' seminar presentations. They are encouraged to write helpful comments and critiques. I average the scores before giving the feedback to the students who presented. I typically talk to the students individually about their presentations, and I delay giving them their feedback until I can schedule private conferences with them. No more than 30 percent of the course grade is determined in this manner. One concern I have had about this approach is the lack of variability in scores students are willing to give one another and the lack of immediate feedback this system caused.

> *They felt uncomfortable about their peer-reviews being part of their peers' grades.*

This year I decided to further explore the dynamics of peer-review. While keeping the written reviews, I initiated discussion in class about students' preferences regarding peer-review. We talked about their experiences with peer-review in their discipline (nursing). What were the most professional approaches to peer-review they had experienced? What supports were needed to make it both meaningful and positive? Face-to-face peer-review where the evaluators are accountable for their feedback was seen as the most professional model. While this approach could bring interpersonal discomfort, having a facilitator present (the professor or a designated peer) provided sufficient support.

I asked what they would like to accomplish with peer-review and what would be the best method of achieving that end. Students overwhelmingly wanted direct and immediate discussion of how the presentation had gone. They specifically wanted to know from their peers what they had done that was helpful and what was not. Did they want to have an impact on peers' course grades? They felt uncomfortable about their peer-reviews being part of their peers' grades. They wanted me to do the grading and felt their job was to give specific feedback that could boost the student's performance.

Because of this feedback in class, we immediately planned to change peer-review for their final presentations. I would do the grading of the presentations. They would take five minutes in class after each presentation to give specific feedback. Did they want ground rules? The only ground rules needed were treating one another with mutual respect and communicating honestly.

I have learned from this experience that immediate feedback is the most important component of peer-review. It needs to occur with openness, honesty, and accountability. Facing one's peers directly and giving constructive criticism is a growth experience for all involved. Facilitating the evolution to direct peer-review has been an enriching growth experience for me as well.

Mary Fisher, Nursing, IUPUI

Quizzes to end classroom silence

In the large literature class, individuals hoped to remain invisible by melting into the crowd. Discussion openers about the reading assignment were met with a chorus of silence. Was I posing inappropriate questions, or had weekend festivities prevented the whole class from reading the piece?

Eventually some students responded, but the general level of awareness remained untested. Help came from a device that, while looking both primitive and petty, soon exerted substantial positive influence on the course. For the remainder of the semester, we were to expect a very brief quiz at the beginning of each session. There would be four multiple-choice items about details of the reading for the day. The object was not to test conceptual understanding and interpretation, but merely the recall of detail. Answers would be easy for anyone who had read the text, and impossible if one had merely been told what it was about. What did the lovers share for dinner? a green apple? a fish she had just caught? old bread? nothing? Or, how many children did they have in later years? one? two? 12? none?

At first I was concerned that students would resent being treated as immature kids. The actual effect, however, was quite different. From then on, people were in their seats before class. If some came late, it was considered a favor if I still let them take the little slip. Discussion improved markedly. I was asked for specific explanations, and we unwrapped and illuminated the significance of detail. Above all, students learned to read with attention. They discovered that they had been cruising the pages on automatic pilot. Respect for the material soared. And when another challenge from me was met with silence, the fault was likely to be mine. Before long, what began as an *ad hoc* adjustment became a regular feature of courses with frequent reading assignments. Course evaluations never criticize the practice but consistently rank class preparation among the highest on campus (96th percentile or higher).

Albrecht Holschuh, Germanic Studies, IU Bloomington

Writing across the curriculum: peer-critique

Like many faculty, when I first began teaching, I just assumed that teaching writing was the responsibility of the English department and to be taken care of in Freshman Comp. As a result, in my upper-level sociology courses, I would regularly assign some kind of term paper at the beginning of the semester and ask the students to turn in the completed assignment some time near the end, with little discussion of it in between. Unfortunately, I often found the results to be unsatisfactory. Not only was I disappointed with my students' efforts, but I was frustrated with my own sense of incompetence and inadequacy in reading and responding to their writing. Fortunately, I was able to consult some very good faculty members in our writing program and from them picked up the use of peer-critiques.

For each course in which I assign a term paper, textual analysis, or book review, I break the assignment down into several segments, including three drafts. A one-paragraph topic statement is due in the second or third week of class and a bibliography two weeks later. I ask for a completed rough draft just after midsemester. However, I do not look at this first draft, but have students trade papers and do a peer-critique using a peer-critique sheet, handed out and discussed in class. The sheet asks students to critique both the intellectual processing and writing of the paper.

Peer-critique sheet: term paper
Intellectual processing

    1. In a few sentences list the major theme(s), topics, and points the author identifies and analyzes in the paper.

    2. How clearly are they articulated by the author (i.e. did you understand them)? What could make them more clear?

    3. What details or evidence does the author use to make these points? Are these materials adequate?

    4. How logically organized is the paper?

    5. In one or two sentences, list the strengths and the weaknesses of the analysis.

    6. What are some steps the writer might take to improve it?

Writing

    1. What part of the paper seems to you the best written? Specify the lines and tell why you feel they are effective.

    2. What part of the paper seems to you the weakest? Specify the lines and tell why you feel they are ineffective.

    3. Which transitions bring you up short and/or leave you searching for connections between sentences or paragraphs?

    4. Which words or phrases are vague and/or overused?

    5. Which sentences have grammatical structures you find confusing or inaccurate?

    6. What spelling and punctuation errors have you noticed?

(Adopted from Peter Schiff, "Responding to Writing: Peer Critiques, Teacher-Student Conferences, and Essay Evaluation," in *Language Connections: Writing and Reading Across the Curriculum.* Urbana, IL: National Council of Teachers of English, 1982.)

While the actual peer-critiques are uneven in quality and detail, the most important element of this exercise is not just the feedback students receive on their individual papers, but also the fact that they must put themselves in the role of the professor in relationship to their own work. They learned this first through their critique of a peer's paper, and they carry it over to their own once they get it back and must make revisions for the second draft. Students then turn in the second draft, the peer-critique, and their first draft to me. I give a detailed review of the second draft, also based on the questions on the peer-critique sheet. The final revision is due at the end of the semester along with copies of the earlier drafts, peer-critique, and my review.

> **Students must put themselves in the role of the professor in relationship to their own work.**

This procedure is relatively easy to implement. It encourages students to see writing as an ongoing process across the curriculum and revision as more than just correcting spelling and punctuation. It also helps them to become more critical and self-reflective readers of their own writing. Using it, I have found a significant improvement in the quality of final papers, I have become much more confident in my reading and response to student writing, and unexpectedly, I have become a much more discerning reader and editor of my own writing.

Mike F. Keen, Sociology, IU South Bend

Reduce test stress: Use exam cards

To provide a relaxing experience for the student both in the examination process and in the review for it, I encourage each student to use a 5 x 7 card. On the card, students can write any mathematical formulas, statistics, and tables that they think might help. I have found that this dramatically lessens students' anxiety. It helps a student to get organized and be better prepared for a test. By the time the semester is over, each student will have several of these 5 x 7 cards, which are useful for quick review for examinations like the GRE and other purposes.

Morteza Shafii-Mousavi, Mathematics and Computer Science, IU South Bend

Assessment of student learning by teachers

Grades are both an incentive for, and a block to, learning. Given the foibles of human nature, nearly all of us, teachers and students alike, seem to need tangible rewards and punishments. Grades fit these categories. They are convenient symbols in the vast and disparate expanse of academic bureaucracy, they serve graduate and professional school entrance committees, and they support the decisions of potential employers outside and inside academia. But they are also obstacles to learning. For most students and, I am afraid, their parents, they have become ends in themselves. They result in grade-hunting, choosing courses that are likely to ensure a good grade rather than an intellectual experience, cramming for examinations, various forms of corner-cutting, and even cheating. Examinations themselves, in order to be easily gradable in large numbers, become tools of semi-scientific (pseudo-scientific?) assessment that assume the mantle of objectivity but do little to reflect the whole student. The old tradition of oral examinations—which when carried out by sensitive, experienced professionals, entails a more humane, holistic assessment—has almost vanished in our wholesale culture.

> *[Grades] are also obstacles to learning. For most students and, I am afraid, their parents, they have become ends in themselves.*

A welcome antidote to this devolution has been the creation of limited enrollment seminars that give beginning students a sense of identity and that allow time for interaction. Small classes of 12 to 15 freshmen and sophomores in the Honors Division where I have taught continually for the last 12 years have enabled me to do entirely away with tests, examinations, and (almost) with formal grades. For formal grades I have substituted detailed critical comments on the six to eight intellectually challenging essays that the students write during the semester. I use every opportunity to further explore the significance of my evaluations in individually scheduled conferences.

This venture is not without drawbacks. To be sure, the students seem deliriously happy, at first, not to constantly run the grade gauntlet and to be able to concentrate on their intellectual exploration, orally and in writing. They discover the challenging joys of true learning. They have a feeling of responsible liberation from a distorting system. Since I teach literature, a holistic enterprise, the material lends itself to the approach.

96

And nothing pleases me more than to hear or read, in evaluations at the end of the semester, that students have not only learned for learning's sake but for life.

But there is also the all too human craving for security, for tangible certainty that begins to gnaw at students around midterm time. They will come in, hem and haw a bit, and finally say: "Mr. Remak, I really enjoy the freedom from formal tests and examinations, but—can't you give me a clearer indication where I stand at this time?" (That really means: "Please, oh please, give me at least an approximate grade!") I do not flinch but point to the substantive comments on their oral and written work I have made throughout the semester. I remind the students that, once out of college and the university, they will have to cope with non-formal, non-number, non-letter evaluations throughout their professional lives. They seem assuaged for the moment, but I sense that the deep-down anxiety for some is real and accentuated by the constant presence and threat in their other academic work, of tests, examinations, and grades.

And I am not exempted from that anxiety myself, for I must follow university regulations that compel me to translate, at the end of the semester, my differentiated assessments of students into cold, bare letter grades (even when they are good, and for Honors students most are good). I also have to keep in mind that this rather daring approach may not work with all or even most "regular" students. Nor does it spare me from the quandary I share with most of my colleagues, grade inflation.

What I do know is that once the semester grades are behind them, the students grow more positive about the challenging, uncertain, but also internally satisfying growing experience they have been through. Helping students to graduate expeditiously is not the *alpha* and *omega* of college. Rather the objective is to enable them to reach their fullest intellectual potential.

Henry H. H. Remak, Germanic Studies, IU Bloomington

Assessment of teachers by students

I have voluntarily employed student evaluations of instruction throughout my teaching career, but they have at least two drawbacks: 1) They come too late to be ploughed back into the course. 2) The fill-in forms are usually so superficial as to be intellectually insulting to both professors and students. They are little more than popularity polls dressed up as "scientific" quantifications.

So I have designed my own (specimen follows). It mentions a number of aspects of the course students might keep in mind as they express their reactions in their own words, anonymously. The evaluation page is distributed two weeks before the semester ends, and students are repeatedly reminded that if they want a real input into the quality of teaching at this university (as they and their elected representatives assiduously profess), they ought to be willing to take the time (20 minutes or so) to write down their observations and recommendations.

The return is seldom what it should be; it is usually 60 to 70 percent. I could raise it if I had them write the evaluations in class, but I have resisted that for several reasons:

1. If students do not care enough about the quality of their education to write down some reactions when urged and given suitable pointers, they do not deserve to be heard.

2. Class time is precious to me.

3. There is something coercive, test-like in being told by the teacher to complete an evaluation in class, precisely what we need to get away from.

4. For the same reason, I do not embrace the policy of an esteemed colleague who presents the evaluation of the teacher as a class assignment and gives his students an "Incomplete" until they turn it in.

5. I want students to think about such an important matter, and to write, at the "right" moment for them, without being "under the clock."

The unsigned, preferably not handwritten assessments, are handed in by each student, directly to one previously designated student who puts them immediately into a large envelope and takes them, after the last class session, to the undergraduate secretary of my department, who is instructed not to give them to me until I have turned in all the grades. Occasionally a latecomer will bring an individual evaluation directly to the secretary.

Subsequently I photocopy them for my files and consult them, from time to time, when I offer the same or a related course again. The originals—all of them—go, voluntarily, to the chair of the department or division. I have found these assessments, by and large, honest, fair, and helpful, but not a substitute for peer-evaluation.

Some years ago, on my campus, an inquiry was made of alums to ascertain their reactions to teachers they had had, if I can recall correctly, three, five, and 10 years previously. It also asked them, specifically, which teachers had taught them most in retrospect, regardless of how they liked them at the time. The results were striking. The tough teachers of yesteryear had taught them more than the "nicer" ones. Solid substance and personal warmth are, we know, by no means incompatible, but it is true that our present culture seems so wrapped up in the cult of instantaneous gratification that we need the corrective of subsequent, more enduring assessments.

Sample student evaluation form

Student evaluations of instruction are particularly valuable in Honors courses because we can count on thoughtful and articulate feedback. PLEASE take the time to think about the following considerations, then comment on all or any of them in your own words. Type your comments, if at all possible. Do not sign! Your comments will be handed to a designated student who will be willing to put them into the envelope provided and hand it, personally, to one of the department secretaries, who will not hand it to the instructor until the course grades have been filed.

Please DO NOT FORGET!!! Thank you, and good luck.

1. From which of the texts did you learn the most (not necessarily those you liked the most)? Which should we consider omitting? Any texts you would wish to add?

2. What did you think of the overall focus? Do you have any suggestions for another overall "theme"?

3. In what way were your attitudes and opinions held at the beginning of the course changed? Or reinforced?

4. What do you think of the overall organization of the course? Should the instructor and/or the students have talked less or more? Can you suggest additional ways in secur-

ing more active student participation beyond just "talking"? Should we have had examinations? More or fewer essays? Other forms of writing? Longer? Shorter? Do you feel you had the opportunity to participate (whether you chose to do so or not)?

5. Any comments on the instructional style and "philosophy"?

6. What ideas did you pick up in the course on which you might wish to work later on?

7. Overall reaction to the course, any further suggestions.

Henry H. H. Remak, Germanic Studies, IU Bloomington

Collaborative exams

In an intensive course in which the majority of the assignments had been accomplished through collaborative work groups, I recently tried collaborative assessment. For the final exam, I gave students four comprehensive essay questions. Each question was similar in scope and difficulty, and each was worth the same points. Students were asked to bring to class (on the day of the exam) a set of two outlines for each question. One set they turned in to me; the other they used as a basis for discussing their responses within their assigned groups. In addition to the four question outlines, each student was to write one individual question. They had the choice of outlining this question prior to the exam day.

> *Students said they learned and conceptualized differently as a result of the group discussion.*

On exam day, I assigned the students to their groups. The groups then met for an hour to discuss their outlines, deliberate over the different perspectives they brought to the question/answer and decide among themselves who would write the group response. Each writer of the group response was to check back with his or her group to make sure the response corresponded to the group's view. I asked that all names be put on the group response and that the author identify herself or himself. Each student also wrote a response to her or his individual question; one-third of the points were given for the question, two-thirds of the points for the completeness of the response.

Students' reactions: Students said they learned and conceptualized differently as a result of the group discussion.

My response: I believe students learned more from this experience than from traditional testing methods. They had to articulate their understanding as well as present views of others. I had individual data from each student (outlines and individual questions and answers), as well as collective responses to evaluate each student's understanding of the material.

Carol S. Browne, Education, IU East

Self-graded student participation

Because I am firmly convinced that participation in class discussion facilitates learning, I make discussion 10 percent of the final course grade in each of my classes. To encourage students to accept responsibility for their own participation, I have each student grade himself or herself at the end of each class session on a four-point scale:

0 = Absent

1 = Present but did not verbally participate

2 = Verbally participated one time

3 = Verbally participated more than once

4 = Contributed my "fair share" to discussion in terms of both quality and quantity

I reserve the right as instructor to assign a student a "5" for participation beyond the call of duty. This occurs only in unusual circumstances such as when a student has taken unusual risks of vulnerability in sharing personal experiences that contribute to an understanding of the material or when a student has shared additional research or reading in response to something that sparked interest in the assigned pages.

In general, I find students will give themselves the same grade that I would have given them. In the event a particular class has a tendency toward inflating their grades, I periodically remind them of the scale and the criteria for assigning grades. When students discover that 10 percent of their course grade is under their complete control, they tend to take participation in discussion seriously and come prepared for each class session.

Jay Howard, Sociology, IUPU Columbus

Multiple-choice, multiple insights

For many years I have held a strong antipathy toward multiple-choice tests, and I dare say that many of my English department colleagues share my feelings. Despite these misgivings, I have found that such tests, if constructed and administered with a mix of rigor and archness, can contribute markedly to the learning process. Let me offer two examples from one test among many that I have devised for a great variety of literary texts.

The multiple-choice quiz, despite its bad reputation, can be used to spark focused, insightful discussion.

When teaching Thoreau's *Walden*, I urge my students, as preparation for their reading of chapter one, to be patient, tolerant, and thoughtful in responding to the different "tricks of rhetoric" (as Emerson called them) that Thoreau used to engage and provoke his readers; these include puns, hyperbole, paradox, along with an excruciating attention to detail, and an assumed superiority to the rest of us who "lead lives of quiet desperation." I also remind students about the non-threatening multiple-choice quiz they will be asked to take over the material.

The quiz is short (usually eight to 10 questions), and I ask students to complete it within five minutes before exchanging papers with their neighbors. I explain that the exercise is meant to shed light on *Walden*, not merely to see who has read well. Two sample questions follow:

1. To begin his experiment, Thoreau borrowed:

   a. one hundred dollars

   b. a compass

   c. an axe

   d. insect repellent

   e. nothing at all

2. Thoreau built most of his cabin out of:
    a. sheet metal
    b. granite
    c. new boards
    d. secondhand boards
    e. none of these

As students grade one another's quizzes, we discuss the ways in which each choice ("a" through "e") falls within or outside the Thoreauvian spirit and context. We then address the issue of how a firm grasp of the "facts" offered by Thoreau is crucial to understanding his rhetorical and metaphorical strategies—how, for example, his elaborate justification for borrowing an axe gives new, radical meanings to such conventional, monetary terms as "most generous" and "interest," or how his many boasts of self-reliance are qualified (he is not a primitivist) by a readiness to acknowledge his dependency on manufactured goods belonging to his neighbors. As for secondhand boards, our discussion leads us to some important conclusions about how both a *practical* and *symbolic* process is being depicted in Thoreau's meticulous description of setting those boards on the grass "to bleach and warp back again in the sun."

In short, the multiple-choice quiz, despite its bad reputation, can be used to spark focused, insightful discussion, while imbuing students with a keen appreciation for the fruits of close, creative reading.

Lewis H. Miller, Jr., Honors Division and English, IU Bloomington

Using counter-arguments for assessment

I use group exercises to do assessments at the close of a unit. This technique promotes active learning and would probably work for you if you have been teaching students about different theories to explain data, different philosophical systems, or different kinds of rhetorical arguments. Basically, you first create a series of brief factual hypotheticals. You then ask the students to come up with the counter-argument, counter-theory, or other criticisms to the one presented in the hypothetical. Each hypothetical should be no longer than a paragraph so that you can review a number of them in a single class period.

You can then assign the students to groups. I have them count off by however many problems I have and make them move around the classroom to form into groups. I can get through at least eight groups in a class period of 75 minutes.

The groups get 10 minutes to come up with their counter-arguments and must write them on overhead transparencies. A spokesperson for the group explains the hypothetical and the theory it illustrates to the class and then explains the group's counter-theory or counter-argument, with help from the rest of the group if there are questions. I then critique the group's work for the benefit of the rest of the class.

In my Law and Public Affairs course for non-lawyers, I use the exercise to get students conversant with the rules of statutory construction, which are often contradictory maxims and tie-breakers for interpreting ambiguous text. For example, if a statute contains a list of objects (cars, trucks, and buses), but it does not list motorcycles, one could apply the rule *to express one is to exclude the other*, and reason that the statute does not cover motorcycles. On the other hand, if the statute pertains to cars, trucks, buses, and

101

other motorized vehicles with wheels, one might use the *ejusdem generis* rule to argue it applies to motorcycles, because there is a catch-all phrase at the end of the list, and motorcycles are of the same class or kinds as the others specifically named in the list. Other rules include plain language, which requires that one interpret a statute consistent with the ordinary meaning of the words. One might also look to the purpose of the statute and the problems the legislature intended it to address.

I give students one-paragraph cases with a few facts, a statute, and a court decision applying a particular rule. These are actual cases from a reading assignment, and they illustrate how courts have used various rules. The students then have to write the appeal and come up with rules of statutory construction that lead to the opposite result. By reviewing each group's work on the overhead with the whole class, I can determine how well the class in general understands the rules and can correct misapplications as we go. By doing this exercise, the students identify most of the typical moves lawyers will make on both sides of an argument over how to interpret a statute.

We do this exercise after we have worked with the rules to the point where students have good recognition-knowledge of them. The exercise tests their ability to apply what they have learned to a new context and to use it critically. Students can do the same kind of exercise on an essay exam and do it in class for a review session. The key to the assessment component is that students have to do something new with information they recognize and have to learn how to criticize and identify the weaknesses or counter-arguments to a particular theory or account that they have previously accepted as gospel. If they can apply a theory appropriately to a new context, or a new data set, or use it to critique someone else's account or explanation for certain results, then they truly understand the theory.

Lisa Bingham, School of Public and Environmental Affairs, IU Bloomington

Recording class participation

Recording and rewarding class participation in large classes can be difficult, yet students often respond well when they know they are held accountable. Rather than calling roll, I pass around a folder during class with a grid containing students' names and class dates. Students initial themselves in. The folder can also be used to return students' papers (grades on the back for privacy) rather than using class time to call names. Other convenient uses of the folder include sending around informational material on related campus events, support services, and so forth.

Scott Sernau, Sociology, IU South Bend

Assessing basic skills of a discipline

Once I began to shift my focus from teaching to learning, I realized that I had mechanisms for testing what my students had learned about my subject matter, history, but none to determine whether they were learning the more basic thinking skills assumed in upper-level courses in my discipline.

Therefore, I created an exercise in which I asked students to perform some of these skills. In the first part of the exercise, I presented students with a passage from a secondary source and asked them to summarize the passage and to separate those elements that would be useful in answering a specific essay question from those that were irrelevant. In the second part, I gave students two passages by historians who offered opposite interpretations of a series of events. Students were asked to compare and contrast the two interpretations and to determine which of a series of evidence would support each position. I then produced a parallel assignment using different passages and labeled the exercises "A" and "B." Since I wanted to measure the increase in my students' ability to do basic historical operations and not their knowledge of the subject matter that I would be teaching, I carefully chose passages that dealt with material that I would not be covering.

> *I wanted to measure the increase in my students' ability to do basic historical operations and not their knowledge of the subject matter.*

On the first day of a large freshman class, I randomly gave half the students exercise "A" and the remainder exercise "B." They each put their name on the exercise, and at the end of the semester I was able to repeat the experiment, giving each of the students the exercise that they had not taken earlier in the semester.

I will now ask some of my colleagues to read over the exercises. They will not know that the two were taken at different points in time, and they will be asked to grade each student's "A" exercise versus his or her "B" exercise. If a significant number of the students did markedly better on the second exercise, I will be able to determine that they gained in their abilities to perform basic historical operations over the semester. By comparing these results from those from similar exercises in the courses of my colleagues, I should be able to determine whether or not my course is really adding to the learning of my students.

David Pace, History, IU Bloomington

No-penalty quizzes

One practice that I have devised to reduce test anxiety is to give short quizzes over the material we have covered during the previous class (lecture and lab). The quizzes use the same forms of questioning that I use on exams—multiple choice, true/false, matching, and short-answer essay. Each quiz is worth three points. If a student earns at least one point on a quiz, the student can add that point to her or his total points as a bonus.

The practice gives the students an opportunity to become effective in dealing with the kinds of questions I ask before even the first exam. It encourages them to keep up with the material, and it allows both the students and me to become aware of what we thought we taught and learned before the exam. The practice also reduces stress for the student because it is a "no-penalty" system.

Joan Lafuze, Biology, IU East, and Pediatric Hemotology, IUPUI

An assignment/learning/evaluation sheet

I have developed the following sheet that I use with research and writing projects. I hand it out (not filled in) when I assign the projects to help the students focus on what I consider to be the most important components of the learning assignment. I then use the sheet to evaluate the students' written work. All categories carry equal weight. Since studies have shown that most students do not read copious notes written throughout their papers, this works well. Use of this sheet also helps me remain consistent from the beginning to the end of a learning module in the feedback I give students.

LAW AND PUBLIC POLICY
Rosemary O'Leary
Briefing A Legal Case

Student: _____

	Excellent	Very Good	Good	Fair	Poor
Name of Case					
Citation					
Policy Issue					
Facts					
Prior Proceedings					
Legal Issues					
Decisions/Holdings					
Reasonings/Rationale					
Remarks					
Form and Style					
Other (as selected by student)					
COMMENTS:					

Grade: _____

Rosemary O'Leary, School of Public and Environmental Affairs, IU Bloomington

Reducing students' resistance to grades

As a first-year teacher, I made a mistake common to many new faculty. When faced with a few students who seemed more interested in getting extra points than in learning, it was easy to become defensive or feel intimidated. I have long since learned that most students understand or at least tolerate the fact that major graded assignments are key motivators to student learning. Here are some verbal and nonverbal techniques that usually worked to shift students from arguing to an emphasis on the learning process:

1. Give all major assignments in writing well in advance of the due dates.

2. Use evaluation forms that have an objective rating system and a place for brief open-ended comments. Clear criteria on the form serves as a checklist for teacher and student. Grading must reflect competence, scholarly rigor, and fairness.

3. Give each student a blank copy of the evaluation form ahead of time.

4. Put old tests and model projects on library reserve prior to grading. This will help decrease students' performance anxiety while countering their arguments of unfamiliarity with the teacher's evaluation style.

5. State orally in class and indicate on evaluation forms that most discussions about grades earned will be delayed until the following class meeting. This allows time for objective review of work and logical versus emotional responses.

6. Since prompt feedback promotes learning, if possible grade and return assignments the same week they are collected.

7. Unless graded assignments are needed for the current lesson, pass out grades near the end of the class period. This minimizes distraction and prevents those students seeking conflict from negatively monopolizing class time. Students with legitimate concerns will usually linger afterwards to ask questions.

8. Return graded papers and projects in a careful manner that will not compromise students' privacy by exposing their grades to others.

9. When returning graded assignments to students, read and display model answers or projects of excellence from past students. This provides current students with a basis of comparison. This must be done with sensitivity and a focus on learning rather than competition.

10. If a student comes to your office, conflict management skills may be useful. Speak softly and slowly, even if the student does not. Indicate you empathize with feelings of disappointment, yet you must follow specific grading criteria for everyone. Although it happens rarely, have a backup plan for a student who may become uncontrollable.

11. Above all, if there are problems with the assignment format or contents, take responsibility and find ways to solve the problem in a professional and ethical manner.

For many years, these strategies have helped me solve grading challenges proactively and retain students' respect. The focus is where it should be—on using graded assignments as motivators for learning subject matter. Students can also learn to model the teacher's use of high academic standards, forethought, integrity, and conflict management skills.

Dorothy W. K. Ige, Communication, IU Northwest

Is there a Lake Wobegon syndrome?

In the debate over grade inflation, some critics decry the fact that the average grade of college students is not a C but rather between a B and a B-. If C is average, does that mean there is a Lake Wobegon syndrome in which "all the children are above average"? Hardly. The real question should be: What grade is "average"?

Although some might argue that a C should represent "average," the very nature of university rules regarding "good standing" makes that standard impossible. At our university, for example, a student must maintain a C (2.0) average to avoid being on probation. Students who consistently earn less than a 2.0 average are asked to leave this university. Thus, for all practical purposes, among students who are in good standing, the real range of grades is not A (4.0) to F (0.0) with the median at C (2.0) but A (4.0) to C (2.0) with the median at B (3.0). This explains why B (or B-) is regarded as "average" and why grade distributions have remained fairly constant (mostly between a 2.75 and 2.90) for so long.

> **My tip is this: Don't worry about grade inflation. Worry about learning.**

One way to recognize that "average" does not always mean a C is to examine grades among graduate students. If we really believe that C indicates "average," should we then be alarmed that the grade-point average of graduate students is typically between 3.5 and 3.7 (3.56 in 1973-74 and 3.66 in 1995-96 at our university)? Of course not. Most professors understand that graduate students must maintain a 3.0 average (and, in some cases, a 3.3 average) to continue their studies. Consequently, any grade lower than a B, in effect, is equivalent to a sub-par performance. It is, therefore, no surprise that B+ or A- is considered "average" and the grade-point average of graduate students is approximately halfway between the highest possible (A) and lowest acceptable (B) grade.

In short, my tip is this: Don't worry about grade inflation. Worry about learning. Just as most of us do not equate "average" with a grade of C for graduate students, we should not view C as "average" for undergraduates.

Brian Powell, Sociology, IU Bloomington

In lieu of the practice exam

One of the major problems with giving essay exams in freshman classes is that many of the newer students have little or no experience with them. Others have never had to perform on a college level, or even close to it. The result is often a horrifically low grade average on the first examination.

I have experimented with several methods to improve the situation: The first is to give a practice examination on a voluntary basis. When I attempted this, 20 percent or fewer of the classes participated.

More recently I gave a required examination in class followed by a second examination. The second examination was optional, but it was in class time, and all were encouraged to take it. If the students improved their grade on the second examination, that was the only grade that counted for the semester. About 90 percent of the students took the second examination, and the average grade was about 10 percent higher than with the voluntary practice exam. This was successful enough that I plan to do it again.

Paul Scherer, History, IU South Bend

106 Clarifying student expectations about exams

Students in my introductory Earth Sciences class often amaze me with their comments about studying for my examinations. While I think that I have given them sufficient information through class discussion and the course syllabus, some students, especially freshmen, seem to think that the focus of the exam is a complete mystery. To clarify the gap between student and instructor expectations, I've tried using the following three questions once they have completed the first exam:

1. What score do you expect to receive on this first exam?

2. What questions, topics, or content areas did you expect on this exam that were not covered?

3. What questions, topics, or content areas were covered on this exam that you did not expect?

If more than a third of my students report similar confusion, then I conclude that I probably have not been as informative as I think I have been. Otherwise, I tend to focus my attention on helping students become more sophisticated learners and participants in my class. To accomplish this goal, I take a few minutes after returning the exams to ask the more successful students to describe how they prepared for the exam, the time involved, the style of preparation, and the focus of attention.

Student evaluations of the second exam do not seem to reflect as much puzzlement over appropriate preparation. This strategy only takes a few minutes in class and may provide useful information in helping students succeed.

Robert B. Votaw, Geosciences, IU Northwest

Stress-free practical exams

One of the problems associated with laboratory courses in the health sciences are the timed intervals at any one station on practical examinations. They often create stress. To reduce the students' anxiety, I tried not timing the practicals and asking the students to take the time they needed at each station and then look up at me when they were finished. When all had finished, I then told them to move on to the next station. I left time at the end for students to return to one or two stations if they needed one more look. Not only did instituting this practice reduce stress for the students, but the remarkable result to me was that it did *not* add to the time of the practical test; on the contrary, students frequently did not take as much time as was designated in the timed tests.

Joan Lafuze, Biology, IU East, and Pediatric Hemotology, IUPUI

No whining: The value of one-page appeals

For 25 years of teaching I struggled to separate feedback on exams from appeals for a change of grade. In consultations in my office, students would try to make a case for a change of grade, while I sought to steer the conversations back to the subject of what the student needed to do differently on the next exam. The result was often satisfying to neither of us.

Then in a discussion of student-faculty interactions in my graduate course on Teaching College History, one of the students, Vince Comerchero, came up with a solution to my problem. Why not make a rule, he suggested, that all students seeking a reconsideration of their grade must present their ideas in a one-page essay? Then the process of feedback would be separated from appeals for changes in the grade, and at the same time students would be reminded of the importance of writing.

This procedure has worked beautifully. I promise students that their comments will be read very carefully and that I will reread the exam foregrounding what they have written. In those classes in which I have graders, this process has the added advantage of allowing all of us who are involved in grading to reconsider a grade collectively in a manner that does not undercut the authority of the graders.

David Pace, History, IU Bloomington

Student-teacher snail-mail

To handle all of the paperwork in a course in which I give out a number of class handouts and in which I either quiz or test every class period, I instituted an "envelope" system.

At the beginning of each semester I obtain enough large manila envelopes for every student. I enclose an index card and distribute one to each student. I instruct the students to put vital information on the index card (name, address, telephone number, major, year in school, and any other personal information they wish to share). On the opposite side, I instruct them to put any information they want me to know about how they learn, what they appreciate in a teacher and any concerns they might have about the semester.

> *I begin with each student an extra communication system that is confidential.*

Then I instruct them to put the card back in the envelope. On the outside of the envelope, I put a label (sticker) where the return address goes and a mailing label on the front. I instruct the students to put the row and seat number on the return label and to address the envelope to themselves using the mailing label.

Thus, I begin with each student an extra communication system that is confidential. I can put graded papers, handouts and/or personal notes in the envelope, and the student can put completed tests, quizzes, and assignments in the envelope for me to collect. Sometimes students will put personal notes regarding a need for a letter of reference, a problem related to class, or a relevant article related to class discussion. One student put pertinent cartoons in several times during the semester.

I use carbon paper to make a copy of my grade sheet for each student (I keep a separate sheet for each one); I can then put that back in the envelope for the student each time. This practice allows the student to know what I have in my grade book at all times. This system helps both the student and me to manage all hard copy for the course and to add another dimension to our communication.

Joan Lafuze, Biology, IU East, and Pediatric Hemotology, IUPUI

Mini-journals

I have incorporated a strategy into my classes that enhances student learning and promotes retention of knowledge. I call this technique "mini-journaling," and it entails distributing a colorful 5 x 8 index card (a different color each class period) to each student five to 10 minutes before the end of class. I ask students to reflect on the content covered that day and write on the card two or three sentences about a concept (or concepts) that

they really understood from the class period and also two or three sentences about a concept (or concepts) that they were still unclear about.

Prior to the next lecture, I review these cards and get a sense of what the class as a whole was able to grasp from the lecture and what they were not. A quick tally of the responses can identify the concept that the greatest number of students were unclear about. For example, in one class, 16 out of 27 students (about 60 percent) wrote that they were still unclear about the pathophysiological changes that lead to compartment syndrome. Based on their responses, I began the following lecture by readdressing this topic, having had time to review additional information and develop a different approach to presenting the content.

This technique provides the student who is afraid to admit in front of the whole class that he or she doesn't understand something the opportunity to get clarification. In addition, it helps me as a teacher know what did and did not "get across" to the students. Lastly, it gives me an opportunity to use a different approach to presenting content that may be difficult for students to grasp. It also conveys to the students that I am interested enough in them to make sure that they understand the lecture material.

Linda Rooda, Nursing, IU Northwest

Uncovering prior knowledge

Research in the field of science education has found that students possess well-established ideas and notions about natural phenomena that are inconsistent with those of scientists. These studies have made me realize how important it is to listen carefully to my students and to provide them with opportunities that reveal their preconceived ideas before launching into new topics.

Over the years, I have learned some simple strategies to help uncover my students' prior "knowledge." Some of the most common techniques I use include the following:

1. Start with a question. Ask students questions pertaining to the specific topic that is going to be presented. For example, for a lesson on physical change, hold up a piece of paper and have the students describe its appearance. Then crush it into a ball and have the students describe its appearance. Ask: How is the paper different now that it has been crushed? How is it the same?

2. Making predictions. Ask students to make predictions related to a specific concept. For example, for a lesson on gravity, hold two objects of different mass at the same distance from the ground. Ask: Will they both hit the ground at the same time? Or, will one arrive before the other?

> *It also is very important to be nonjudgmental of students' responses.*

3. Notecard writing. Have students write on one side of a 3 x 5 notecard what they know about the main topics that are going to be presented in the next unit of instruction. These cards could also be used at the end of the unit to assess what changes occurred in the students' understanding of the main topics of the units.

4. Brainstorming. Have students share as much as they know about the main topic(s) to be presented during the next class session.

5. Concept maps. Ask students to make a concept map the main ideas of the unit. Sometimes this strategy is also referred to as developing "mind maps" or "graphic organizers." For a good resource on concept maps, see J. D. Novak and D. B. Gowin, 1984. *Learning How to Learn.* New York: Cambridge University Press.

When using these strategies, it's important you allow ample time for student responses and dialogue. It also is very important to be nonjudgmental of students' responses. The main purpose of these techniques is to gain insight into your students' prior knowledge. In so doing, you are provided with data to help modify your instruction, and you simultaneously allow your students to *reflect* on the things they do and do not understand about a specific topic.

Charles Barman, Education, IUPUI

What did you learn today?

What learning goes on in the classroom with our well-designed discussions, presentations, and structured activities? That's the big question in higher education today. But on a very small scale, I am often curious about what the students think about the time we spend in class and their improved understanding of the content. I also wonder how rapidly they take on the more sophisticated learning strategies I attempt to nurture. So, I have been asking my students in our introductory earth science class to tell me a bit about what happened in class today. The following two questions can be answered in a few minutes at the end of class and have been especially helpful in discovering the problems that arise in understanding, particularly when "big" ideas are presented and discussed.

1. What did you learn today that was interesting and that you would like to learn more about?

2. What did you hear in class today that was confusing or unclear?

Robert B. Votaw, Geosciences, IU Northwest

Thumbs up or thumbs down

Whenever I teach a large class, I monitor the nonverbal behavior of my students and ask questions throughout the lecture or discussion to check for responses to the concepts being presented. However, these methods do not always give me good feedback on how well all students are understanding the material.

A strategy I have observed in public schools and have adapted for large-group teaching is the "Thumbs Up or Thumbs Down" technique. Early in the semester, I give my students instructions on how to use "Thumbs Up or Thumbs Down." During a presentation, I will periodically stop and "ask to see a thumb." Students have been instructed to hold a closed fist next to their body and, if they understand what has been presented, to stick up a thumb. If students are not sure whether they understand the concept, then the thumbs are pointed down. No thumbs pointed up or down indicate the students are not sure whether they understand what is being presented.

A quick survey of thumbs will help me determine how well students understand my presentation. With a high number of thumbs up (students understand), I can continue the presentation as planned. However, if many students present no thumb (students are undecided) or thumbs down (students do not understand), I then can ask some probing questions to determine where there is a need for further discussion or explanation.

Thumbs Up	**Thumbs Down**	**Closed fist**
Student understands concept being taught	Student does not understand concept	Student is not sure if he/she understands concept

This technique allows each student in a large group presentation to give me immediate input on understanding. By monitoring this feedback, I can adjust my presentations to promote more student learning.

John C. Moody, Education, IU Southeast

The one-minute paper

Over the past few years, I have used the "one-minute paper" in my classes and have observed some very positive effects. The concept and the method I use for this teaching strategy is straightforward. During each lecture, I stop the class for a few minutes and request students to write down answer(s) to the question(s) I ask. These questions are about the main concepts from the lecture up to that point. Then, I go around and review everybody's answer. This works rather well in small to medium-sized classes. An option for large classes is to collect and return them to the students, with feedback if you wish, at the next class.

This evidence of the students' abilities, or lack of abilities, to express the main point(s) of a lecture provides me with a sense of how well they are understanding the topic. I then respond to these promptly and try to address and clarify the areas of confusion. This rapid feedback keeps the class on track and provides me with an opportunity to correct misconceptions before they become fairly established. Another benefit of the "one-minute paper" is to help entice students away from passive note-taking toward more active learning. In my opinion, students become more confident as learners and feel more connected to the instructor.

> *Another benefit of the one-minute paper is to help entice students away from passive note taking toward more active learning.*

Atilla Tuncay, Chemistry, IU Northwest

Optional assignments

Some of the most popular and useful assignments for my students have been optional assignments that allow them to apply course material or explore additional areas of interest. A certain number of options or option-points can be assigned, or students can improve their grade totals by selecting from a series of optional assignments. These have included noting and commenting on class-related material in newspapers, magazines, television, and film; participating in class-related community activities and commenting on insights gained; and making personal applications of course material.

I ask that all options be short, allow a variety of formats, and allow a certain number of cumulative optional points that can be added to the students' totals when figuring grades.

The options allow students to partially compensate for a poor test performance or assignment. More important, they encourage students to make the link between class content and what they see and do in the rest of their lives.

A benefit for me is that I receive a steady stream of course-related materials to help me stay current with popular media and community activities when my own time to gather them is limited. Some of best materials can be shared with the class as examples, handouts, or discussion topics.

Scott Sernau, Sociology, IU South Bend

Grading exams fairly

Since I give predominantly essay examinations in most courses, I have experimented with a variety of means to reduce the subjective element in grading. What I have found to be the single most effective device is to grade in a manner that makes it impossible for me to know whose examination I am grading.

> *If I am in a good or bad mood, tired or awake, it does not affect an entire examination result, but is the same for the entire class on that one question.*

I achieve this by opening up all of the exams so that the cover (with names, etc.) does not show. Then I proceed to grade one question for the entire class before moving on to the next question. This allows me to compare the results for the entire class on that one question before moving on to the next one. This has added value that if I am in a good or bad mood, tired or awake, it does not affect an entire examination result, but is the same for the entire class on that one question. Otherwise, if I grade, shall we say, 10 exams at one time and another 20 the next day, the conditions of my mood or physical state can unconsciously influence the results.

Without some such technique, it is virtually impossible to avoid at least some subconscious prejudices to influence the results.

Paul Scherer, History, IU South Bend

Instant feedback on exams

Prompt feedback can be an important part of making an exam a learning activity. My current strategy is this: On objective tests, students circle answers on the test pages. They then transfer these answers to a Scantron sheet, which they turn in, keeping the test pages. When all are finished, we go over the test in class. Students receive two added points for making corrections on the test pages and turning these in. This way students leave knowing their test grade and, more important, seeing immediately what they did right and wrong, while the test is still fresh in their minds. I can then keep the test pages so they are not circulating in case there are late makeups.

Scott Sernau, Sociology, IU South Bend

112

Peer-evaluation of teaching

In my nearly six decades of college and university teaching, I have found that nothing draws so suspiciously quick and defensive a rejection as my conviction that we will never make classroom teaching equal with published research in the reward structure until we devise a viable, substantive system of peer-evaluation. Student feedback is helpful but much more relevant to instructional presentation and personality than to intellectual substance and scholarly command of the field. Copies of course synopses, handouts, and examinations are complementary evidence and relevant, but cannot take the place of the real thing: actual oral teaching. Filming our own classes gives us a more immediate picture of what we do right, wrong, or in between, but it cannot focus on more than one angle of the class at one time.

Teaching is not a private privilege brooking no "external" intrusion. It is a primary, contractual obligation. No matter how long we resist it, the question is not whether peer-evaluation of teaching will be done but whether we will be able to shape its implementation with competence, tact, and sensitivity rather than having it imposed on us. The prevailing practice of the chair visiting a faculty member up for tenure once or twice for the embellishment of a tenure dossier is tokenism, if not hypocrisy.

What has worked best in my experience is the following arrangement:

1. Several years before the tenure decision, four faculty members (but it also works for two or three), two tenured seniors and two untenured juniors, who are compatible with each other and share genuine intellectual and pedagogical interest in the subject matter, get together and agree to visit each other. (A deft chair can sometimes be helpful in bringing them together.) The initiative may come from either side. The auditing days selected, by previous consent, should reflect a characteristic aspect of the course. Optimally there are two or three consecutive visits to place the treatment of a particular topic into a rounded, reasonably coherent context.

2. We take a few notes in class to remind us of interesting intellectual or instructional items lending themselves to future conversation, but otherwise we watch, listen, and enjoy this intellectual experience like any other. We may take more notes, after class on our own, to serve as memory joggers for future discussion.

3. After the first two, three, or four visits (mutual) we get together for a good, leisurely lunch and just talk. Nothing formal, just the kind of relaxed, intellectual but informal social discourse that is, alas, languishing in today's larger universities, regretted by almost all, restored by few.

4. Having lunch (good food and drink promote good conversation) around the middle of the semester has the advantage of being potentially fruitful for the rest of the instructional semester, on all sides.

5. The same informal procedure is repeated in the second part of the semester; juniors visiting seniors, seniors visiting juniors.

6. At the end of the semester, we get together again for lunch and continue to talk.

7. The seniors then tell the juniors that if the younger contingent wants the senior partner to write a formal letter for subsequent inclusion in their dossiers, the senior would be pleased to do so. The senior partner is, of course, free to excuse herself or himself for whatever reason, and the junior partner may not request such a letter.

8. If it has worked, the same senior/junior partnership may be repeated subsequently for different courses. Or partners on either side may team up with different colleagues. The faculty need not belong to the same department; nowadays we often find colleagues in other departments with interests and competencies closer to our own or with personalities more compatible than those we find in our own departments.

> *It is, of course, not perfect. Perfection is an excuse for inaction.*

The advantages to this arrangement are:

1. It has a constituent of real mutuality.

2. It reduces if it does not totally eliminate the invidious, self-conscious, and even discriminatory (seniors visit juniors but are not visited) flavor from the auditing and brings it back toward what is, or should be, the foundation of an intellectual community.

3. It is far more informative about the total teaching personality of instructors/scholars than the current practices.

4. It has flexibility; it can be inaugurated and shaped by both sides at any time.

5. It has the element of voluntarism but it also responds, whether you like them or not, to the academic facts of life (recognition, reappointment, promotion, tenure, career).

It is, of course, not perfect. Perfection is an excuse for inaction.

Henry H. H. Remak, Germanic Studies, IU Bloomington

114

Quick wits

Inspired teachers . . . cannot be ordered by the gross from the factory. They must be discovered, one by one, and brought home from the woods and swamps like orchids. They must be placed in a conservatory, not in a carpenter-shop, and they must be honored and trusted.

John Jay Chapman

You can pay people to teach, but not to care.

Marva Collins

Please remember these two difficult truths of teaching:
1. No matter how much you do, you'll feel it's not enough.
2. Just because you can only do a little is no excuse for doing nothing.

Susan Ohanian

Since we can't know what knowledge will be most needed in the future, it is senseless to try to teach it in advance. Instead, we should try to turn out people who love learning so much and learn so well that they will be able to learn whatever needs to be learned.

John Holt

We're drowning in information and starving for knowledge.

Rutherford D. Rogers

It is not only by the questions we have answered that progress may be measured, but also by those we are still asking. The passionate controversies of one era are viewed as sterile preoccupations by another, for knowledge alters what we seek as well as what we find.

Freda Adler

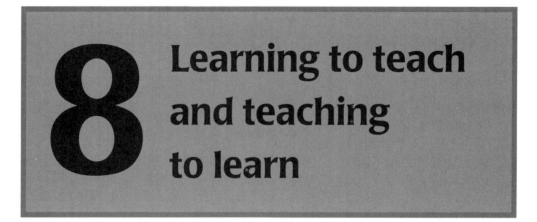

8 Learning to teach and teaching to learn

Students aren't the only ones who have a lot to learn. So do teachers. And the best teachers are learning all the time. But how? We learn by reflecting on our experiences. We learn from our students. We learn from mistakes. We learn by finding mentors. We learn from books and from one another. We also teach to learn, knowing that some of the deepest learning comes through teaching. Knowing this, we may even ask our students to teach so they too can experience both the growth and satisfaction of learning by teaching.

Taking the risk to team-teach

Although we are in the same discipline, philosophy, we had never taught together. As partners, we had often discussed philosophical issues—we had even published a joint paper a few years before—but we had never worked together in the classroom.

One reason is that our specific fields diverged, with one's interests in the philosophy of art and the other's in the philosophy of mind and metaphysics. More dramatically, one's approach was multidisciplinary, reaching into gender studies, art criticism, and art history; the other's was analytical, using the traditional tools of logic and argument.

The main reason we have not taught together, however, is that we felt we knew each other too well! Often in team-teaching, one sees an opportunity to learn about and from another faculty member. Knowing each other's views as well as we did, as both marital partners and intellectual colleagues, presented the risk that exploration might give way to in-class disagreement. We feared that disagreement—as opposed to normal give-and-take—would confuse the students in a way that inhibited learning.

However, when we had the opportunity to teach seniors enrolled in a special university program for outstanding undergraduate scholars, we decided to take the risk. Since we both enjoyed the outdoors and had often talked about the sublimity of nature when hiking, we agreed to focus the course on "the beautiful and the sublime."

The seminar of 20 upper-division students met weekly at our home on the campus grounds. We added to the informality of the meeting place by serving coffee (highly appreciated, given the early morning class time) and by inviting our golden retriever to sit in on the class. We decided to alternate leading the class, with one being the lead presenter while the other occasionally asked questions and made comments; then we would reverse roles. We would rehearse somewhat, but mostly the class interactions were spontaneous.

Our reading list was eclectic, to put it mildly. The course began with Edmund Burke's 18th-century treatise on beauty and the sublime and included readings from traditional American nature writers, contemporary analytic philosophers, and writers and artists focused on contemporary culture. We showed slides, mostly of the grand paintings of J. M. W. Turner, and included several musical presentations. There were two field trips, one to a museum of art, and one to a majestic renovation of a historic hotel.

The students were wonderful. They brought significant intelligence and experience to the class meetings, including what they had learned while studying abroad. Sometimes we thought that the best we could do was introduce the subject, provide

> *Sometimes we thought that the best we could do was introduce the subject, provide a little background, and get out of the way.*

a little background, and get out of the way. It was the ideal situation; the students were teaching each other, engaging the material and working through difficult concepts, primarily on their own. They motivated each other—and us—to work toward a definition of the "sublime" that grew out of the readings and paintings.

The students' evaluations were revealing. We were pleased that they were highly complimentary, but there was one repeated constructive criticism: The students wished

117

that we would have disagreed with each other more than we did. Assuming that the students were not simply goading us to argue, their point was that they learned best from intellectual risk-taking and a willingness to explore contrasting perspectives. Contrary to our initial concern that disagreement would inhibit class learning, we discovered that students, at least upper-class ones, have a high tolerance for disagreement among members of a faculty team, provided that the disagreement is intellectually honest.

We look forward to team-teaching again sometime. Although we had talked philosophy for years, we found that the class situations, especially the interactions with the students, enlivened and challenged our perspectives on each other's approaches. The class moved us beyond the standard answers we had been giving to each other's positions to deeper levels. The risk paid off, and we learned that team-teaching could be productive and satisfying, not only to students, but to one another.

**Myles Brand, IU President and Philosophy,
and Peg Brand, Philosophy and Gender Studies, IU Bloomington**

Team-teaching with your eyes open

For some time, I had hankered to try my hand at team-teaching. Then I fell into conversation with a teacher at our university's medical school about his own team-teaching experience. How was it? I wanted to know.

"Terrible," he said, "At least at first. But then it got better. . . . If you are going to team-teach," this teacher advised, "go into it with your eyes open. Don't expect the experience to save you time—it doesn't. Just because there are two of you does not mean you will have half the work; sometimes you will have twice the work, at least initially, until you work out all the kinks. . . . There will be discomfort, too, in the classroom," he said. "Your styles will be different. You will disagree on what is important. You will want to take different approaches to the same topic. It will, in short, be HARD."

"Well, then," I asked. "Is it worth it?" Absolutely, he replied. He and his colleague had been team-teaching the same course now for five or six years, and after about the third iteration, it had grown easy. These team-teachers were convinced that what the students were getting from the two of them together was far superior to what they would have gotten from either of them individually. Moreover, these two teachers had become good friends.

> 'There will be discomfort, too, in the classroom,' he said. 'It will, in short, be HARD.'

I have never forgotten those words and conveyed them to a colleague who approached me to team-teach a class last year. We should not do this, I said, because we think it will involve less work—it won't. We should not do this because we think it will be easier—it won't be. We should do this because we want to move beyond "same ol', same ol'" to challenge ourselves and our students, and because we want to get to know one another better, as friends and colleagues. We agreed to team-teach in that spirit.

Needless to say, problems arose during the semester. There were differences of style and expectations that caused mutual exasperation and often required time-consuming

118

negotiation. There was an unexpected diffusion of responsibility that often left strings untied. In a spirit of compromise, there were times when we each felt we were doing things we weren't really sure about. But we prevailed. In the main, we were not thrown by the problems; we had expected difficulties, and we dealt with them. Moreover, when a deeply troubling plagiarism issue arose in the class, we had twice the emotional resources to deal with the problem.

In the end, we agreed: We had not only created an interesting course, but we had grown much closer as colleagues and friends. In an era where burnout in the academy is commonplace and community is hard to come by, this was no small accomplishment.

S. Holly Stocking, Journalism, IU Bloomington

From my teachers I have learned

From my own teachers, I have learned many things, including a few unwritten values on learning and teaching.

• From a professor who served as a role model, I learned the value of modeling for my students.

• From well-prepared and punctual professors, I learned the value of preparedness and punctuality.

• From concerned professors, I learned the value of caring for students.

• From an arrogant professor, I learned the value of being down to earth.

• From a professor who humiliated me in front of my classmates, I learned the value of respect for students.

• From an unavailable research professor, I learned the value of availability to students.

• From a boring professor, I learned the value of enthusiasm and excitement about teaching.

• From a professor with high expectations, I learned the value of high academic standards.

• From a professor who read from the textbook, I learned the value of lecture and discussion beyond the textbook.

• From a professor who was insensitive to ethnicity, I learned the value of cultural sensitivity.

• From a monotonous professor, I learned the value of using a variety of instructional strategies.

• From a talkative teacher, I learned the value of listening to students.

• From a professor who forgot what it is like to be a student, I learned the value of sitting in on classes.

• From irrelevant courses, I learned the value of personalizing my courses.

• From students' expressions, I learned the value of self-evaluation.

• From rigid and inflexible professors, I learned the value of sensitivity to students' needs.

• From long and dull lectures, I learned the value of punctuating my lectures with humor and cartoons.

• From a professor who said one thing and did another, I learned the value of practicing what you preach.

119

• Finally, from the success of my former students, I learned the value of teaching.

Mohammad Torabi, Applied Health Science, IU Bloomington

'I teach people'

Some of my best teachers were crusty old sergeants in the U. S. Army. During the spring of 1966 in Advanced Infantry Training at Fort Jackson, S.C., several of us were chatting on a break with Sergeant First Class Don Williamson. Some of my classmates had been teachers in civilian life, and the topic turned to teaching. "What did you teach?" Williamson asked them. "History," said one. "Math," said another. "Physics," volunteered a third. And on it went. When the question had circumnavigated the group, Williamson delivered his punch line. "I'm different from all of you," he declared. "I teach people!"

It was a crystallizing comment that put learning and teaching in perspective in my thinking. At some point, I linked Williamson's insight with an etymology lesson taught by Miss Eileen Johnson, my high school Latin teacher. She explained that "instruct" came from a Latin verb *instruere*, which means to put information into a person, while "educate" came from *educare*, which means to elicit discovery from a person. She left no doubt which kind of teaching she thought was superior. Several years later, my wife, Joyce McMahan Cookman, who at that time was a high school teacher, was given a framed quotation from Kahlil Gibran. I think it expresses the same idea:

> A wise teacher does not bid you enter the house of his wisdom, but rather leads you to the threshold of your own mind.

Claude Cookman, Journalism, IU Bloomington

Prepping for essay exams

After my first year of teaching undergraduates, I realized that my means of assessing students' knowledge did not correspond to my teaching philosophy. I was devising multiple-choice exams that were weighted heavily with factual knowledge, yet I wanted students to go beyond mere memorization of the course content. I wanted them to be able to discuss the material, compare and contrast different positions, and defend a thesis with evidence.

The next semester, I revised my first exam to be what I considered a thought-provoking short-essay exam. I remember reading over the first set of exams with a growing horror. The students had treated each essay question as an opportunity to write down everything they had memorized on a given topic. Often they had not addressed the question at all. I spent the next class period discussing the exam with the class. It became clear to me that most of the students did not understand what I had wanted them to do. I had not done an adequate job preparing them to take this type of exam. Their honest response led to a number of positive class changes.

I now assign a weekly journal question (often "old" exam questions) that serve as a prototype to my exam. Students write an answer to the question, and I give them short written feedback. I also use class activities that require the class to write mock exam questions. We discuss ways to document an opinion with evidence, and I remind the students of the difference between an opinion based on data and one based on personal preference.

In other words, I now teach the strategies for writing short-essay exams. It is the least I can do.

Barbara Fazio, Speech and Hearing Sciences, IU Bloomington

Training teachers through peer-mentoring

We often talk about our students as our "companions in learning," and we complain that students direct too many of their comments to us while rarely talking among themselves. Complaints aside, most of us still do lecture perhaps more than we should and, in countless other ways, set ourselves up as experts. Only once in a while do we come up with ways of actually building peer-learning into our classes.

For about 20 years, I have worked with teacher-training in the Department of Speech Communication. For most of those years, I did the training myself. Then, three years ago, I heard the graduate students in my teacher-training course talk about how they had picked up a great idea for teaching this or that concept from an experienced associate instructor. I thought that this collaboration was great but sensed that it was also pretty much hit and miss. I decided that I would try to incorporate collaborative learning into my teacher-training class by starting a peer-mentoring program.

Here's what the program involves. First, in the summer, I invite all experienced associate instructors (AIs) in Speech Communication to volunteer to serve as mentors. To qualify as mentors, they have to be willing to do the following:

1. Prepare a brief (one-page) written description of two or three activities that have worked really well for them in teaching a public speaking course that is taught by all first-year AIs. I compile these and distribute them to newcomers during orientation week.

2. Visit my teacher-training course at least once to use some of these strategies—to present a favorite mini-lecture, discuss their philosophy of teaching, describe a real teaching challenge they once encountered and how they handled it, or discuss how to balance life as a graduate student with life as an AI.

3. Allow my teacher-training students to visit the AIs' own classrooms to observe them teach. These observations are arranged in advance. Each student in my teacher-training course observes three peer-mentors and writes a brief statement of what he or she learned about teaching from the observation.

> *Most of us still do lecture perhaps more than we should and, in countless other ways, set ourselves up as experts.*

4. Participate in a few social events—typically held at my home—to encourage new and returning AIs to become better acquainted informally.

Besides these basic activities, some peer-mentors who have gone on to other teaching experiences (such as teaching Business and Professional Communication) visit the class and describe their perceptions of these other courses and how they are similar to or different from teaching basic public speaking courses. Other peer-mentors who are starting

121

to enter the job market join us for a special session on building the teaching portfolio, and they offer advice and share some of their experiences.

Through the peer-mentoring program, I have had the chance to see students who are sharing, listening to, and truly valuing their senior peers' ideas about teaching. I have discovered that, while I may know quite a bit about teacher-training, I am not a graduate teaching assistant. Their challenges and perspectives may differ from mine; thankfully, they also differ from one another's. From the peer-mentors, the new associate instructors learn that there are many different styles of teaching and many different ways of enacting effective teaching, and I am reminded that commitments to teaching and teaching excellence are widely distributed among my young colleagues. With their help, the AI training program in speech communication has become a venture in collaborative learning.

Patricia Hayes Andrews, Speech Communication, IU Bloomington

No pat on the back in order

Some years ago, I was teaching a two-semester course in my discipline. The first semester, my attention was drawn to a student in his late 20s or early 30s who asked good questions in class and who obviously understood the material. The trouble was that neither his tests nor his papers reflected his ability. I wrote him long notes on all his work, hoping to get him on track. In the middle of the second semester, he handed in a paper that was obviously first class, and I wrote nice things all over it. Secretly, of course, I was patting myself on the back, figuring that my mentoring had played a big part in his improvement. After I returned the papers and everyone was filing out of the classroom, this student was one of the last to leave. He had been going over my comments, and I noticed that he was smiling. "Would you like to know why I did so well on this paper?" he asked. "Of course," I answered expectantly. "I got laid off at work," he replied.

Roy Schreiber, History, IU South Bend

Less teaching, more learning?

I learned a powerful lesson about student evaluation a decade or more ago. I was teaching a course in which we trained upper-class students to be advising peers for incoming freshmen. The course required copious amounts of learning of facts and some synthesizing into a larger picture.

Year after year, I received outstanding evaluations based on my lectures, demos, diagrams, histrionics, and the like, but alas, the students performed miserably when we unleashed them on the freshmen.

Unhappy, I wrote a small textbook in which the burden shifted from my "teaching" to the students' learning, because students had to do exercise after exercise that I rigorously graded. Passing the course was contingent upon a 90 percent grade with no adjusting of grades based on the distribution of scores.

Everyone passed. The competence of the student staff soared. The freshmen were helped. My course evaluations plummeted.

I wonder if there is a message there anywhere?

Philip W. Namy, Education, IU Bloomington

General rules for enthusiasm

Research indicates that professors and courses both are rated more positively by students when the instructor is perceived to be "enthusiastic" about the subject matter and about teaching. However, a review of the teaching literature reveals little specific information on this important teaching quality. In 1994, I facilitated a brainstorming session at the Second Post-Lilly Teaching Fellows Retreat at the University of Wisconsin-Parkside on this topic. Below is a summary of the questions and answers that emerged when small groups discussed this issue and when the groups met again together.

How can we communicate enthusiasm about our subject and our teaching to students?

- by coming early to class and staying after class
- by being prepared
- by acting glad to be there
- by showing empathy toward students
- by respecting the length of their attention spans (for example, most people drift off after 10 minutes of straight talk or lecture)
- by varying the pitch and intensity of our voices
- by giving students responsibility for their own learning
- by not having preconceived notions about the subject matter or students' abilities that set a pessimistic tone in the classroom (for example, "x" majors have to take this class, and they aren't up to it)

How can we sustain our enthusiasm about teaching after years of teaching, especially of the same course?

- by reconnecting with what got us into this to start with (for example, attending conferences to stimulate new learning, developing research projects related to our teaching assignments)
- by talking about teaching with colleagues and sharing ideas about how to better use class time and solve problems we have
- by taking risks and teaching new courses, trying new assignments
- by practicing good time-management skills so that we have time to do other things we enjoy in our work and leisure time
- by finding ways to retain and communicate our own passion for learning (for example, using our research as examples in the classroom)
- by attending workshops and reading literature on teaching to learn more about how students learn.

How can we establish a classroom that encourages students to be enthusiastic participants in the learning process?

- by understanding that students have diverse learning styles and strengths
- by learning more about and bringing into the course the interests and expertise of our students
- by creating an environment, expectations, and assignments that encourage students

to take an active responsibility for their own learning (for example, by focusing on real-life problems for students to solve)

• by setting up learning opportunities that encourage students to collaborate and learn from one another

• by connecting learning to students' lives outside the classroom

What help do we need in developing or maintaining our enthusiasm for the teaching-learning enterprise?

• technology, equipment, and classroom layouts that support diverse teaching and learning styles

• workshops, sabbaticals, and grants to improve teaching

• greater variety of feedback from students (for example, graduating student surveys and one-minute response cards completed by students after each class)

• non-evaluative peer- and expert-reviews of our teaching

Linda Haas, Sociology, IUPUI

Evaluating ourselves

At the end of each class session, I ask myself the following questions:

1. Did students learn something new?
2. Was I prepared enough for this session?
3. If I were a student, would I want to have a teacher like me?
4. Did the session fit well with the overall course objectives?

Then, I give myself a grade A, B, C, D, or F for my overall teaching performance that day. If my grade is less than a B, I ask myself why and try to improve for the next session. If the grade for my teaching performance is an A, I ask myself why, so I can retain the skill factors that contributed to my success. At the end of the semester, I compare my overall grade with my best students' grades and hope for a strong correlation. Through self-evaluation, I can see the big picture, which includes having access to students every day, student evaluations, eye contact with students, my own knowledge of the subject, my history of teaching, and my sense of strength and limitations.

Mohammad R. Torabi, Applied Health Science, IU Bloomington

Engaging associate instructors in the course

For eight semesters, I have taught a large lecture course with four or five associate instructors (AIs). I have found the best way to get their involvement is to include them in the planning of the course and the design of its teaching materials. I also invite them—on a voluntary basis—to give presentations and mini-lectures before the entire class on topics of their expertise. I include short biographies and photographs of them in the syllabus, introduce them on the first day of class, and generally try to ensure that all the students in the course know all the AIs, not just their discussion leader.

Semester after semester, AIs in my course have shown the greatest anxiety over grading. I have tried to allay their uncertainties by using the same method my supervising professors used when I was a graduate student leading a discussion section. Each section leader skims his or her assignments and selects the two best, the two worst and two in the middle. We meet and compare our students' work across sections, eventually establishing the points at which a C+ becomes a B, a B becomes a B+, and so forth. We also discuss how best to phrase our written feedback.

For AIs who are still uncertain, I have a standing offer to review with them any work for which they feel uncomfortable assigning a grade. Generally, one or two sessions are all they need to gain confidence in the grading process and their judgements.

> *The best way to get AIs' involvement is to include them in the planning of the course and the design of its teaching materials.*

Additional touches, such as gatherings at the professor's house or end-of-the-semester meals at a restaurant help solidify the bonds between professor and associate instructor. I also make it a practice to write a letter for each AI's file, detailing her or his contribution to the teaching mission of the course.

It is a commonplace for teachers to say they learn from their students. Some of my most important lessons about teaching have come from associate instructors. What I have gained from them far outweighs any time or effort I have expended in "managing" this resource.

Claude Cookman, Journalism, IU Bloomington

What associate instructors need to know

Faculty members who work with associate instructors (AIs) have an obligation to help them develop into good teachers, both for their own benefit and for that of the undergraduates in the course. For a large lecture course to succeed, the professor in charge must ensure that all AIs heading discussion sections know the course content, subscribe to the course objectives, embrace the philosophy of teaching and learning, understand the grading criteria, and master the pertinent teaching skills, which may range from math and language instruction to conducting discussions and demonstrating laboratory methods.

The best way to accomplish this is with straightforward communication. Associate instructors cannot meet our expectations if we do not communicate them clearly. Here's a short check list of items that should be made clear before the course begins and reiterated throughout the semester:

1. Your teaching philosophy
2. Your objectives for the course and the learning climate you want to establish
3. How you plan to achieve those objectives and that climate
4. Your expectations about the AIs' general role
5. Your expectations about the AIs' specific duties and deadlines
6. When during the semester the AIs can expect periods of intense work
7. Clear and specific criteria for grading student work

Claude Cookman, Journalism, IU Bloomington

A hit is a hit is a hit (Not!)

A few years ago after I started teaching, I came across strategies for teaching that I thought were brilliant. Developed as part of the University of Arizona Medical School's Curriculum on Medical Ignorance, these strategies involve teaching students how to recognize, accept, and manage ignorance. In the Tucson program, doctors-in-training keep "ignorance logs" where they track what they personally don't know about medicine, and what doctors collectively don't know about the body, diseases, treatments, medical policy, and ethics. They write "ignorance papers," papers about what isn't known—a very different kind of paper from the usual term paper that covers what medical researchers believe is known. Students listen to "visiting professors of ignorance" discuss the role of ignorance in their own lives as medical researchers and clinicians.

The approach struck me as dazzlingly innovative and exactly what the doctor ordered for journalists-in-training who must routinely confront and manage their own ignorance. Indeed, so excited was I about these strategies for my own students in the School of Journalism that I visited the Curriculum on Medical Ignorance, observed what was being done, and immediately upon my return to my own campus, put the strategies into practice. Propelled more by enthusiasm than good sense, I adopted these innovations almost whole-cloth, only to discover within a few short weeks that what worked easily for medical students was not going to work so easily for a very different student population attempting to learn very different material. Even worse, I attempted to adopt these strategies in an untried course with an untried text. Students quickly got confused and anxious, as did I. The rest of the semester was an exercise in trying to make a difficult situation tolerable—for all of us.

> **What I learned from this experience was to adopt innovations a little less breathlessly.**

What I learned from this experience was to adopt innovations a little less breathlessly. New pedagogical tools are best implemented with a sensitivity to difference in student populations. They are best put into practice in tried-and-true courses, gradually and with forethought. What works well in one setting could be a disaster in another. Try new things, yes, yes. Just try them using a little wisdom. It was a painful lesson, but one that, in the years since, has stood me in good stead.

S. Holly Stocking, Journalism, IU Bloomington

A new look at class preparation

One day I found myself walking into a classroom to run a literary discussion without having read the assigned story. I was not proud of myself. Never before, in 20 years of teaching, had I been in this situation. Guilt and the potential for shame were rivaled only by the practical question of what to do with the next 75 minutes.

Close to panic in the front of the room, I was saved by a tiny voice of survival that whispered in my ear, "We need to be creative here. So, what's the difference, really, whether you have read the story or not?" The hopeful answer seemed to be "Nothing I can't work with." I went ahead to preside over one of the best discussions I had ever had.

What happened? Basically, I think, even if for the wrong reason, I did the right thing: I got myself out of the way—that is, the confusing part of myself, the "expert" in the front of the room. I put myself instead in the role of a friend who wanted to know more about a story he hadn't read, asking first for basic information about the story, then asking for the students' interpretations, evaluations, and cultural connections.

Of course, these are the things we always do. The difference was that this discussion wasn't confused by the students' wondering about some right answer that I was sitting on in the front of the room. There wasn't any. They were the "experts," and I was the one needing their expertise. That simplicity changed everything. Volunteering was nonstop, and there was a constant interplay between the students as they quickly and naturally did the double-checking and refinement they needed to be the good "experts" they (naturally) wanted to be.

> *This discussion wasn't confused by the students' wondering about some right answer that I was sitting on in the front of the room.*

No, I didn't stop preparing for classes, but since that near-disaster, I have tried to design pedagogical equivalents of my lack of preparation that would recreate the clarity, simplicity, and eager participation of that suddenly empowered group of students.

John Woodcock, English, IU Bloomington

Students teaching teachers

A great idea for a teaching retreat: Ask students to teach you something.

I recently did this, asking four dance students to teach hip hop to the gathered teachers.

Two weeks before the retreat, in an effort to understand the abilities of their future "students," the dancers attempted to teach some of the steps to me—a fiftysomething dance-challenged female. In a hallway in the student union, with hip hop music blasting from a portable CD player, the students tried to show me what to do.

My first efforts to imitate the steps were agony. I felt awkward. I could not keep the sequence straight. The movements I did make seemed all wrong. I was blushing from embarrassment.

One of the students, seeing my distress, began to break down the sequence of steps, into smaller and smaller units. Another reassured me that there was no one way to dance hip hop. A third said "Just listen to the beat, move with the beat."

I began to relax. That night I not only began to learn hip hop, but I rediscovered the wisdom of students, and in a way that would have been impossible for me without becoming a student again myself, I learned about good teaching as well.

S. Holly Stocking, Journalism, IU Bloomington

FOILed again

Some years ago, I was teaching an introductory class of about 90 students. The subject matter was bioanthropology, in which genetics and evolution form a considerable part. Many students whose prior experience with simple algebra raised uncomfortable feelings now found themselves having to relive this agony when I began to work through a problem in binomial expansion, that is *(p + q) (p + q)*. Over the years, my attempts to adequately explain the binomial expansion proved woefully inadequate.

> **When I just can't seem to get my points across, I seek assistance from the class.**

Then, one day in class, it happened. As I methodically plied the chalkboard with *p x p* and *p x q*, etc., I heard a murmur run through the students, finally reaching my ears as FOIL. I repeated aloud this apparently magical word, which was followed by an enthusiastic and knowing echo from the class. For the moment, I was baffled as to how this simple word somehow explained what I had so struggled to teach. A student in the front row volunteered to come to the chalkboard. She worked a problem, in FOIL fashion, to the applause of her appreciative colleagues.

My carry-home lesson was this. What I thought was simple was actually complicated by a time differential in our educational experiences. I had not heard of FOIL until that day, yet it was a seemingly revered aid to learning binomial expansion. In all subsequent classes, I now use the mnemonic. But the lesson broadens. There have been other similar situations in which I just can't seem to get my points across, and so I seek assistance from the class. It is often said that knowledge is accumulative and additive. This FOIL lesson tells me that comprehension and understanding may well be interactive and multiplicative. Simply stated, if, in a binomial expression, the algebraic terms are *Teachers* and *Learners*, then comprehension comes by expanding *(T + L) (T + L)*. Kindly use FOIL.

Robert Meier, Anthropology, IU Bloomington

The critical reading guide

The critical reading guide has helped me and my students work on mastery of important concepts, on development of classroom discussion of topics of interest, on the ethical implications of the advancement of science, on improvement of their writing, on selection of important concepts, and on critical thinking. This idea seems so simple that I wonder why it took me 25 years to think of it.

The critical reading guide for each chapter or reading assignment is a single sheet of paper, labeled with the chapter to which it applies, a place for the student's name, and seven questions with space for answers.

Questions 1 to 5 ask for the students' written descriptions of their understanding of key points or major concepts in the reading assignment.

The last two questions on the reading guide are always the same:

6. What topics or concepts do you understand from reading the chapter?

7. What topics or concepts are unclear or difficult to understand from reading the chapter?

Here are points of value for your students and for you, the instructor, in the development of your own critical reading guide:

1. Students receive the critical reading guide with the reading assignment.

2. Students are informed that the critical reading guide, with their written comments, will be collected at the beginning of class and graded ($\sqrt{+}$, 0, $\sqrt{-}$). They receive points for attempting to answer the questions on the guide. These points create "value" for them since the points are part of their grades in the course. The students are graded on preparation for class and on their effort to understand the important topics—not just on the correctness of their answers.

3. The questions focus on the important issues and concepts in the reading assignment. These questions help the student know which issues or topics are important in my view.

4. Essay questions on each exam are taken from the questions on the critical reading guide. The students now have an opportunity to practice writing answers to important questions and to know which questions are important.

5. Students indicate on the critical reading guide which topics are easy to master. Thus, they inform me of those topics that do not need any further discussion.

6. Students indicate on the critical reading guide which topics are difficult to master or are poorly understood from their preparation. Consequently, they inform me at the beginning of the class period about topics that should receive attention during the week.

7. Students, on some occasions during class time, are permitted to revise or modify their answers (in red pen) and submit their reading guide at the end of the class period, thus allowing them to show me what they have learned during the class discussion.

8. I check topics that are generally considered to be understood by asking students to write about them in two-minute essays in the following class meetings.

What advantages have I gained from using the critical reading guide?

1. Student attendance and participation may improve as the result of using the critical reading guide.

2. The critical reading guide shifts much more of the responsibility for learning onto my students and allows me, as the instructor, to be a coach, mentor, and nurturer. This may be a shift that is at the core of student learning and development of critical thinking.

> *The critical reading guide shifts much more of the responsibility for learning onto my students and allows me to be a coach, mentor, and nurturer.*

3. Colleagues have expressed a concern that the development and use of the critical reading guide concept creates more work for us, the instructors. The compensation for this additional time, however, can be better student performance on our evaluation of their progress in the course. The critical reading guide has allowed me effectively to replace the 75-minute illustrated lecture by the "Sage on the Stage" with a vibrant class period of student discussion, "sermonettes," writing exercises, and explanations of difficult topics.

Robert B. Votaw, Geosciences, IU Northwest

Learning is a matter of perspective

One way to keep teaching skills honed is to look at things from the learner's perspective. Some teachers always seem to keep the learner's perspective in mind. As they climb the ladder of expertise in their discipline, they seemingly keep one toe on the ground. But others often lose touch with what it was like to be a novice in the field.

> **Some teachers always seem to keep the learner's perspective in mind.**

Several of the finest teachers I've met while serving as director of a faculty development center have practiced their learning skills by taking up a new interest every few years. This enabled them to remember that uncomfortable or even clueless feeling of being a learner new to a subject. One professor learned *T'ai Chi*, another yoga; one man in his 40s learned to drive a car; a 50-something woman joined a choral group. Even Stephen Brookfield, author of *The Skillful Teacher*, wrote of learning to swim in middle age.

When I'm developing instruction or observing someone teach, I personally find it helps to become, for a short time, a learner in that course. I try to understand what is being taught and what I would be required to do as a student. When I get to the point where something is difficult to understand, then I jump into the role of teacher and try to figure out how to improve it.

When I was new to developing instruction, I used to be embarrassed when I would not be able to understand what a professor in an undergraduate course was teaching. I'd gloss over it as I discussed the course with the teacher. Now, the places where I have difficulty understanding are the very ones I zero in on. Being a master learner, jumping back and forth from the role of learner to teacher, is a useful tool for good teaching.

Joan Middendorf, Teaching Resources Center, IU Bloomington

Quick wits

Education in the formal sense is only a part of the society's larger task of abetting the individual's intellectual, emotional, and moral growth. What we must reach for is a conception of perpetual self-discovery, perpetual reshaping to realize one's best self, to be the person one should be.

John W. Gardner

The greatest enemy of understanding is coverage—the compulsion to touch everything in the textbook just because it is there.

Howard Gardner and V. Boix-Mansilla

The things taught in colleges and schools are not an education, but the means of education.

Ralph Waldo Emerson

Nobody starts out as a completely effective and creative teacher. . . . The desire to teach and the ability to teach well are not the same thing. With the rarest of exceptions, one has to learn how to become a good teacher.

Herbert Kohl

All teachers need to have the courage of their contradictions.

Susan Ohanian

Tomorrow's illiterate will not be the man who can't read; he will the man who has not learned how to learn.

Herbert Gerjuoy

No one can become really educated without having pursued some study in which he took no interest—for it is a part of education to learn to interest ourselves in subjects for which we have no aptitude.

T. S. Eliot

9 Quick list: Recommended books on teaching

Teaching tips are helpful. They show us new ways of doing things. Sometimes they even remind us that old ways of doing things are best. But as valuable as they may be, tips are just that—the tips of thoughts that typically go much, much deeper. Many of us, in searching for inspiration and support as teachers, and in developing and refining our own philosophies of teaching and learning, look to works that offer more depth than this one. Such books and articles offer not only "hits" that have worked in a particular class, but knowledge, rationales, and carefully articulated wisdom. In this chapter, a few of us offer a very personal list of books that have deepened us as teachers. We offer this annotated list with an awareness that we have not covered all the books that might offer guidance and sustenance, but with the hope that all readers will discover at least one new work to inform and inspire them and, finding that work, will pass its wisdom on.

O'Reilly, Mary Rose. *The Peaceable Classroom.* Portsmouth, NH: Boynton/Cook
Publishers, 1993.

A teacher of writing at a top-flight liberal arts college told me about this book. She
had found so many useful nuggets of insight in this slim volume that she typed and distributed them to all her teaching friends. To wit: "What if we were to take seriously the
possibility that our students have a rich and authortative inner life, and tried to nourish it
rather than negate it?" And: "You can't just put your chairs in a circle and forget about
the human condition." O'Reilley, a Quaker teacher of English, believes what we do in
the classroom matters deeply to the kinds of people our students will become. It matters
deeply, too, to the kind of society we hope to create. If we allow our students to bring to
the classroom the questions that dominate their lives, we will be in a better position to
help them—and ourselves—find the answers.

S. Holly Stocking, Journalism, IU Bloomington

Palmer, Parker J. *To Know as We are Known: Education as a Spiritual Journey.* San
Francisco: Harper, 1993.

I would buy anything by Parker Palmer. He is a humane educator of educators. He
resists the temptation to separate the head from the heart, and believes in the need to put
the word "love" back into higher education—love of learning, love of subject, love of
students, love of ourselves. For those with spiritual concerns, his is an intelligent guide to
the kind of spirituality that "encourages us to welcome diversity and conflict, to tolerate
ambiguity, and to embrace paradox. By this understanding, the spirituality of education is
not about dictating ends. It is about examining and clarifying the inner sources of teaching and learning, ridding of us the toxins that poison our hearts and minds. . . . Fear, not
ignorance, is the enemy of learning, and that fear is what gives ignorance power." (p. xi)

S. Holly Stocking, Journalism, IU Bloomington

Kroll, Barry M. *Teaching Hearts and Minds: College Students Reflect on the Vietnam
War in Literature.* Carbondale and Edwardsville: Southern Illinois University Press,
1992.

Barry Kroll, former Indiana University professor, is a gifted teacher of literature who
has been profoundly influenced by the thinking of John Dewey. In this volume, Kroll
describes how he makes use of provocative readings, journals, analytical essays, and
small-group discussions to encourage students to grapple with both their emotional and
their intellectual responses to literature about the War in Vietnam. There are no tests in
a Barry Kroll classroom–just thoughtfully designed assignments challenging students to
grapple with what is true, what is right, what is good, and what is beautiful. Kroll seeks
to captivate hearts and minds, and he succeeds brilliantly. As I am a teacher whose temperament and subject matter welcome both reflection and feeling, I found much here to
inspire me.

S. Holly Stocking, Journalism, IU Bloomington

133

Boice, Robert. *First-Order Principles for College Teachers: Ten Basic Ways to Improve The Teaching Process.* Bolton, MA: Anker Publishing, 1997.

This provocative monograph attempts to avoid using old truisms about teaching, and in the process invents some new and interesting ones, which the author considers "first-order principles" in the manner of science. For example, Boice advises the would-be excellent professor to "build resilience by limiting wasted efforts;" "let others do some of the work;" and (good advice, even for many non-teaching occasions) "begin before feeling ready." The author emphasizes the importance of creating a context for learning which includes but is not limited to the classroom (the tongue-in-cheek Boice rule for that is "Moderate classroom incivilities by prosocial immediacies").

Eileen T. Bender, English, IU South Bend

Grasha, Anthony F. *Teaching With Style: A Practical Guide to Enhancing Learning by Understanding Teaching and Learning Styles.* Pittsburgh: Alliance Publishers, 1996.

Those who have been fortunate enough to attend one of Tony Grasha's workshops on teaching and learning styles will find his expansive text (365 pp.) as lively and useful. Generously illustrated with explanatory charts, graphs, anecdotes, and classroom examples, this may be an indispensable handbook for professors who believe the most important key to good teaching is identifying the diverse learning styles of one's students and then incorporating a variety of instructional styles into the course design. Grasha has translated the Myers-Briggs temperament inventory into a detailed "psychological type index" related directly to classroom learning, and he includes it in the beginning of the book for an instructor to use or adapt. But understanding student learning styles is only the beginning. His sections which follow on teaching styles and strategies to promote active learning contain enough good ideas to cover virtually any classroom situation. This would also be a valuable reference in a faculty development program.

Eileen T. Bender, English, IU South Bend

Ericson, Betty LaSere, and Diane Weltner Strommer. *Teaching College Freshmen.* San Francisco: Jossey-Bass, 1991.

Although it was written at the beginning of the decade, this text remains useful as a consideration of teaching and learning in the critical freshman year—the year that experts agree often determines a student's collegiate future. Perhaps that is because even in 1991, the authors were not gearing their study to the traditional "freshman" alone. Thus, this text deals interestingly and constructively with issues affecting the persistence and success of a variety of student groups in nonresidential as well as residential settings. Some issues cross Carnegie "categories": how to promote active learning, how to reach students even in large classes, and how to respond to the beginning student who typically needs to learn how to learn and is still a "dualist" in the Perry scheme of cognitive development. The chapter on assessment and evaluation is particularly useful.

Eileen T. Bender, English, IU South Bend

Rose, Mike. *Lives on The Boundary: The Struggles and Achievements of America's Underprepared.* New York: Free Press, 1989.

This text has taught me more than decades of teaching "non-traditional" students about the underlying motivations, assumptions, and concerns of those students and the gap between their expectations and experiences and those of their professors. Rose, who was himself an "underprepared" student coming to UCLA from one of the poorest neighborhoods in Los Angeles, uses his autobiography as a case study of the collegiate experience of the urban poor. The final chapters, in which he reflects on the problems and provides a framework for possible solutions, may be the most valuable, particularly "The Politics of Remediation," which could be used as an independent essay by faculty and student service staff discussing student learning and student retention. Since its first printing, there has been a paperback edition reasonably priced for faculty, staff, and student use.

Eileen T. Bender, English, IU South Bend

Tobias, Sheila. *They're Not Dumb, They're Just Different.* Tucson, AZ: Research Corporation, 1990.

This short monograph makes a strong statement about why able students are "turned off" by science as currently taught in many post-secondary institutions. The research study by Tobias, better known for her earlier *Overcoming Math Anxiety*, excoriates certain faculty for their inflexible attitudes about what makes a "scientist," and outlines the experience of students who turned to the humanities for the kind of engagement and intellectual exploration they had expected but did not find in their science classrooms. While her case studies and examples are drawn from science teaching, the central problem she exposes—the need to recognize different learning styles and promote active learning strategies—is critical to teaching in any discipline. This slim volume may also reassure those readers who once felt lost in a science or mathematics classroom where everyone else seemed to be learning.

Eileen T. Bender, English, IU South Bend

Champagne, Audrey B. and Leslie E. Hornig. *Science Teaching.* Washington, DC: American Association for the Advancement of Science, 1986

While the AAAS has published other annual reports of general interest to faculty, this 1986 collection of essays on the teaching of science is an extraordinarily interesting and lively discussion of the challenges posed by the expansion of classroom technologies and new scientific knowledge and the contraction of government support for scientific research. Contributors to this forum range from Newt Gingrich and Erich Bloch (then head of NSF), commenting on federal policy and funding of science, to teachers and professors reporting from the classroom. The topics are also wide-ranging: effective classroom teaching; the "curriculum-proof teacher"; the need for generalized science literacy; equity and excellence issues; and the impact of science teaching in a "technological world."

Eileen T. Bender, English, IU South Bend

135

Denby, David. *Great Books: My Adventure with Homer, Rousseau, Woolf, and Other Indestructible Writers of the Western World.* New York: Simon and Schuster/ Touchstone, 1996.

A few years ago, David Denby did something many professors fantasize about but few actually do: He returned to college as a student, specifically, to enroll in the "core course" he had once taken as a Columbia University freshman. The result is a text which provokes and sometimes angers, but finally inspires renewed consideration of the "classics" and their relationships to learning and living. Denby is indeed an unusual freshman; he brings a cultural critic's habit of mind to his second look at the "great books," expanding and illuminating the interaction between artist, text, and reader. His readings are enhanced by his ability to embed the study of literature almost seamlessly into life experience—and vice versa. The reader becomes a privileged observer of his conversations and arguments with the writers and works he is studying. Denby is equally open about the events of his "real" life which influence his understanding of texts. Reading a classic like *The Iliad* in the '60s, he had been alienated, acutely uncomfortable about its valorization of war heroes. Rereading it in the '90s, he finds the trappings of middle-class life dull and prosaic compared with the "intoxicating" lines of Homer. Re-reading the classics also gives him a special perspective on his mother's sudden death. Denby's response to Woolf, admiring though it is, contrasts with his dismissive reflections on feminist literature which some may find problematic. Nevertheless, because of its honesty and readerly intelligence, *Great Books* is a remarkable guide to the active, insatiable, well-furnished mind of the "perpetual student."

Eileen T. Bender, English, IU South Bend

Gibaldi, Joseph, Series Editor. *Approaches to Teaching World Literature Series.* New York: Modern Language Association (series 1982–present).

The Modern Language Association has now published almost 45 volumes in this series, each of which contains valuable biographical and contextual materials as well as brief annotated syllabi from on-going courses. Combining "hands-on" reports from the classroom with reliable and solid background readings from a variety of institutional settings makes each volume a valuable addition to the literature professor's shelf. Titles "approached" include classics (e.g., Chaucer, Dante, Cervantes, Voltaire); reading list standards (e.g., *Beowulf, Moby Dick, Faust,* Shelley's Poetry), and books reflecting modern concerns (e.g., *The Awakening, The Way to Rainy Mountain, The Woman Warrior, Things Fall Apart*). It makes sense to check with MLA periodically, since new titles are always in the works.

Eileen T. Bender, English, IU South Bend

Palmer, Parker J. *The Courage to Teach: Exploring the Inner Landscape of a Teacher's Life.* San Francisco, CA: Jossey-Bass, 1998

Exposing the unfulfilled promise of today's university, this book provides both a critique and a more spacious vision of the professoriate. Parker J. Palmer, long a guide to the spiritual dimensions of teaching and learning, approaches the "disconnected life" of faculty—seemingly enforced by the "broken paradoxes" of contemporary higher educa-

tion—with heartening optimism. Challenging persistent myths of individualism and division which create what he calls "a culture of fear," Palmer charts an alternative academic territory. He makes a persuasive case that knowing, learning, and engaging in an ongoing "conversation with colleagues" can transform the "secret" and isolating life of a university teacher into a generative and fulfilling vocation.

Eileen T. Bender, English, IU South Bend

Senge, Peter M. *Leading Learning Organizations: The Bold, The Powerful, and The Invisible.* MIT Center for Organizational Learning, 1995.

In recent decades, universities have looked to the literature of corporate management for theories and strategies of decision-making. In this MIT Center for Organizational Research Monograph, Senge, author of the widely-discussed *The Fifth Discipline: The Art and Practice of The Learning Organization* (Doubleday, 1990), moves the conversation to a different level which recognizes "learning" as the operative principle of organizational leadership. His explorations of models of leadership which are not hierarchical or "top-down," but "individual to individual" and "individual to system" have interesting and provocative implications for the university, and suggest a new role and demand for faculty leadership.

Eileen T. Bender, English, IU South Bend

Hutchings, Pat. *Making Teaching Community Property: A Menu for Peer-Collaboration and Peer-Review.* Washington, DC: American Association for Higher Education, 1996.

Is teaching scholarly work? If so, how should this work be fostered, developed, and assessed? These questions are addressed in this report published by the American Association for Higher Education as part of its ongoing Teaching Initiative. Drawing upon Lee S. Shulman's work on the reintegration of teaching and scholarly activity, the AAHE project is headed by Pat Hutchings, who introduces and is the editor of this useful and interesting volume of case studies, demonstrating the impact of collegial activity on specific disciplines in a variety of institutions.

Eileen T. Bender, English, IU South Bend

Rogers, Carl. *Freedom to Learn.* Columbus, OH: Merrill, 1969.

Carl Rogers was ahead of his time with this classic volume, designed to offer "practical ways of dealing with students which stimulate and facilitate significant and self-reliant learning". Many people enamored of the "new" learning paradigm might be surprised to read how Rogers and others whom he includes in this volume were working successfully with most of these ideas three decades ago. Rogers offers examples of the pursuit of "freedom to learn" and "self-directed learning" at several different levels of education. And he also offers some ways to work with such an approach within a large educational system. I try to incorporate many of his ideas into my teaching and to help students appreciate what I am trying to do. I assign several relevant chapters in the book for them (on reserve in the library) to read during the first weeks of the class. The students are always positively impressed, especially with Rogers' "passionate statement" about graduate education.

J. Vincent Peterson, Division of Education, IU South Bend

Mills, C. Wright. *The Sociological Imagination.* New York: Oxford University Press, 1959.

In trying to make sense of the world, I find this volume particularly useful. A goal of all my courses is to enliven this imagination, which Mills calls the intercept of biography and history. Developing the "sociological imagination" should enable individuals to achieve a more comprehensive and realistic understanding of the historical and institutional forces that underlie the problems they face. Mills notes that often individuals "cannot cope with their personal troubles in such ways as to control the structural transformations that usually lie behind them." According to Mills, the effect of sociological analysis may be both stimulating and liberating:

> By its use men [and women] whose mentalities have swept only a series of limited orbits often come to feel as if suddenly awakened in a house with which they had only supposed to be familiar. Correctly or incorrectly, they often come to feel that they can now provide themselves with adequate summations, cohesive assessments, comprehensive orientations. . . . Their capacity for astonishment is made lively again. (pp. 7-8)

If such a perspective interests you, then reading this book is a must.

Robert Arnove, Education, IU Bloomington

138

Index of contributors

About the editors

S. Holly Stocking is Associate Professor of Journalism at Indiana University, Bloomington. Eileen T. Bender is Professor of English at Indiana University, South Bend, and one of the founders of FACET—The Faculty Colloquium on Excellence in Teaching at Indiana University. Claude H. Cookman is Assistant Professor of Journalism at Indiana University, Bloomington. J. Vincent Peterson is Professor of Education and Program Director of Counseling and Human Services at Indiana University, South Bend. Robert B. Votaw is Associate Professor of Geology and Director of the Academic Resource Center at Indiana University, Northwest. All are members of FACET.

The Faculty Colloquium on Excellence in Teaching (FACET) was established at Indiana Univeristy (IU) in 1989 to recognize and support gifted teachers from each of the eight IU campuses (IU Bloomington; IU East in Richmond; IU Ft. Wayne; IU Kokomo; IU Northwest in Gary; Indiana University–Purdue University, Indianapolis; IU South Bend; and IU Southeast in New Albany), and to provide a forum for the discussion of teaching and university policy. Royalties from this publication will help support FACET activities that promote teaching excellence on the IU campuses.

Index of subjects

The text for *More Quick Hits* is set in Times New Roman. Titles, subheads and other display type are set in Poppl-Laudatio Medium. Quotations are set in Poppl-Ladatio Medium Italic. Book design and pre-press production are by Claude Cookman.